I0008289

Hands-On Test Management with Jira

End-to-end test management with Zephyr, synapseRT, and Jenkins in Jira

Afsana Atar

BIRMINGHAM - MUMBAI

Hands-On Test Management with Jira

Copyright © 2019 Packt Publishing

All rights reserved. No part of this book may be reproduced, stored in a retrieval system, or transmitted in any form or by any means, without the prior written permission of the publisher, except in the case of brief quotations embedded in critical articles or reviews.

Every effort has been made in the preparation of this book to ensure the accuracy of the information presented. However, the information contained in this book is sold without warranty, either express or implied. Neither the author, nor Packt Publishing or its dealers and distributors, will be held liable for any damages caused or alleged to have been caused directly or indirectly by this book.

Packt Publishing has endeavored to provide trademark information about all of the companies and products mentioned in this book by the appropriate use of capitals. However, Packt Publishing cannot guarantee the accuracy of this information.

Commissioning Editor: Kunal Chaudhari
Acquisition Editor: Denim Pinto
Content Development Editor: Ruvika Rao
Technical Editor: Sabaah Navlekar
Copy Editor: Safis Editing
Project Coordinator: Vaidehi Sawant
Proofreader: Safis Editing
Indexer: Manju Arasan
Graphics: Alishon Mendonsa
Production Coordinator: Tom Scaria

First published: February 2019

Production reference: 1150219

Published by Packt Publishing Ltd.
Livery Place
35 Livery Street
Birmingham
B3 2PB, UK.

ISBN 978-1-78995-452-4

www.packtpub.com

To every software project team that wanted to streamline their processes but did not know how to start...

`mapt.io`

Mapt is an online digital library that gives you full access to over 5,000 books and videos, as well as industry leading tools to help you plan your personal development and advance your career. For more information, please visit our website.

Why subscribe?

- Spend less time learning and more time coding with practical eBooks and Videos from over 4,000 industry professionals

- Improve your learning with Skill Plans built especially for you

- Get a free eBook or video every month

- Mapt is fully searchable

- Copy and paste, print, and bookmark content

Packt.com

Did you know that Packt offers eBook versions of every book published, with PDF and ePub files available? You can upgrade to the eBook version at `www.packt.com` and as a print book customer, you are entitled to a discount on the eBook copy. Get in touch with us at `customercare@packtpub.com` for more details.

At `www.packt.com`, you can also read a collection of free technical articles, sign up for a range of free newsletters, and receive exclusive discounts and offers on Packt books and eBooks.

Contributors

About the author

Afsana Atar is an accomplished test engineer with a decade's experience in software testing. She extends her thought leadership to teams in various domains, from digital advertising, education, and healthcare, to the financial sector, insurance, and trading. Previously, she worked with Google, IBM, the Principal Financial Group, and the Children's Hospital of Philadelphia, and is presently working for Susquehanna International Group. She is a Certified Scrum Master, an Agile Scrum practitioner, and is also part of the Scrum Alliance community. She has managed and worked on projects worth over $1M as a QA engineer to a QA manager. She believes in sharing her experiences with the testing community to help foster learning and innovation.

About the reviewer

Varun Pillai is an accomplished technical manager, a seasoned software engineer, and a data scientist with over 10 years' experience in managing multicultural project teams making end-to-end deliveries in SDLC and the Agile-Scrum process for advertising, banking, and insurance companies. He has worked with various MNCs, such as HSBC and the Principal Financial Group. He is currently working with the advertising unit at AlticeUSA.

He is an avid technologist and is always looking to experiment with the next big technology stack for data science. In addition to his work, he also contributes to open source projects and offers consultancy services to start-ups in relation to their technology stacks and business processes.

Packt is searching for authors like you

If you're interested in becoming an author for Packt, please visit `authors.packtpub.com` and apply today. We have worked with thousands of developers and tech professionals, just like you, to help them share their insight with the global tech community. You can make a general application, apply for a specific hot topic that we are recruiting an author for, or submit your own idea.

Table of Contents

Preface

This book will provide a practical understanding of the test management process with Jira. The book presupposes no qualifications on the part of readers trying to streamline their test management processes and will guide you through a step-by-step approach to implementing test management effectively. It focuses on the basic concepts, covering details of the software testing process followed by the organization of test artifacts in Jira. It then explores and contrasts between the three most popular Jira plugins—Zephyr, Test Management, and synapseRT—that are widely used for test management.

Topics covered include creating and managing projects in Jira, creating Jira tickets to manage customer requirements, tracking Jira tickets, creating test plans, test cases, test suites, defects, requirement traceability matrices, and generating reports in Jira. It also covers the best practices for establishing a scalable and effective test management suite in Jira. The book primarily focuses on the following:

- **Familiarizing users with concepts**: The reader starts with learning about software quality assurance thought processes, as well as quality management standards used in the industry, thereby familiarizing themselves with the software development process and phases with the deliverable management generated at each stage of the software development life cycle.
- **Familiarizing users with tools**: The reader will then progress to learn how Jira can be used to organize and manage their Agile projects in Scrum and Kanban. They will also learn about Jira plugins from the Atlassian Marketplace that will help in test management.
- **Understanding the test management approach**: The reader will then learn how to plan and manage workflow as per their project requirements.
- **Learn to implement**: The reader will then learn in detail the best approaches in terms of selecting various project execution workflows based on the needs of the project, as well as learn different aspects of test planning, test strategy, and test execution.
- **Monitoring and controlling project activities**: The reader will then learn how Jira can help in defining strategy, as well as monitoring and controlling projects using different type reports.
- **Continuous integration with Jira and Jenkins**: The reader will then learn how to configure Jira plugins to create, manage, and execute automated test scripts in Jira using Jenkins.

Who this book is for

This book is for any quality assurance professional, software project manager, or test manager interested in learning to implement test management best practices in their team or organization.

What this book covers

Chapter 1, *An Overview of Software Quality Assurance*, explains quality assurance thought processes and quality management standards. It also describes the software life cycle, and familiarizes the reader with the deliverables at each stage of the life cycle.

Chapter 2, *Getting Started with Jira*, covers how Jira can be used to organize and manage our Agile projects in Scrum and Kanban. It also discusses Jira plugins from the Atlassian Marketplace that will help in test management.

Chapter 3, *Understanding Components of Testing with Jira*, covers in detail how each phase of test management can be performed using the test management plugins in Jira. It also compares the features provided by each plugin.

Chapter 4, *Test Management Approach*, covers in detail the best approaches to selecting various project execution workflows based on the needs of the project.

Chapter 5, *Test Planning*, discusses different aspects of test planning and test strategy while understanding the relationship between requirements and the test plan. It also explains how Jira can help us in defining and comparing strategies for our testing needs using the synapseRT, Zephyr, and Test Management tools.

Chapter 6, *Test Design Phase*, explains the process of test case design and creation. It also explains how to organize test cases and hone our skills in reusing test cases and test data.

Chapter 7, *Test Execution Phase*, describes the process of test execution and how it will be managed using Jira.

Chapter 8, *Defect Management Phase*, discusses the importance of defect management and explains how Jira helps us in tracking and managing defects effectively.

Chapter 9, *Requirement Management*, discusses how Jira issues can be used to track project requirements. It also explains ways in which Jira can be used to link requirements with test cases as requirement coverage.

Chapter 10, *Test Execution Status Reporting*, explores how Jira can help monitor and control projects using reports. It details various reports offered by Jira.

Chapter 11, *Jira Integration with Automated Testing Tools*, explores how third-party automated testing tools can be integrated with Jira to manage automated test cases.

To get the most out of this book

We expect readers to understand the basics of the software development process and have some familiarity with Jira. Readers do not need to have any prior knowledge of test management tools, as the book will cover these concepts from the basics through to an advanced level.

To complete this book successfully, readers will require computer systems with at least an Intel Core i3 processor or equivalent, 8 GB RAM, and 4 GB of available storage space. In addition, you will require the following software:

- Windows or iOS operating system.
- Google Chrome / Firefox Mozilla / Internet Explorer (latest version) browsers
- Jira (version 7 onward) with the synaseRT, Zephyr, and Test Management plugins. The version used in this book is 7.
- Jenkins (version 2.150 onward).
- Eclipse IDE.
- Java 8 for Jenkins.

Download the color images

We also provide a PDF file that has color images of the screenshots/diagrams used in this book. You can download it here: https://www.packtpub.com/sites/default/files/downloads/9781789954524_ColorImages.pdf

Conventions used

There are a number of text conventions used throughout this book.

CodeInText: Indicates code words in text, database table names, folder names, filenames, file extensions, pathnames, dummy URLs, user input, and Twitter handles. Here is an example: "Testers may also have to use different types of files, such as .doc, .docx, .txt, .pdf, .xls, .xlsx, .csv, .png, or .jpeg to import the data in order to make sure that it works or doesn't work as defined in the test case."

A block of code is set as follows:

```
package JenkinsDemoPkg;
import org.testng.annotations.Test;
public class demoJenkins {
        @Test
        public void testJenkins(){
                System.out.println("Hello World");
        }
}
```

Bold: Indicates a new term, an important word, or words that you see on screen. For example, words in menus or dialog boxes appear in the text like this. Here is an example: "Let's click on the **Create new project** button."

 Warnings or important notes appear like this.

 Tips and tricks appear like this.

Get in touch

Feedback from our readers is always welcome.

General feedback: If you have questions about any aspect of this book, mention the book title in the subject of your message and email us at customercare@packtpub.com.

Errata: Although we have taken every care to ensure the accuracy of our content, mistakes do happen. If you have found a mistake in this book, we would be grateful if you would report this to us. Please visit www.packt.com/submit-errata, selecting your book, clicking on the Errata Submission Form link, and entering the details.

Piracy: If you come across any illegal copies of our works in any form on the internet, we would be grateful if you would provide us with the location address or website name. Please contact us at copyright@packt.com with a link to the material.

If you are interested in becoming an author: If there is a topic that you have expertise in, and you are interested in either writing or contributing to a book, please visit authors.packtpub.com.

Reviews

Please leave a review. Once you have read and used this book, why not leave a review on the site that you purchased it from? Potential readers can then see and use your unbiased opinion to make purchase decisions, we at Packt can understand what you think about our products, and our authors can see your feedback on their book. Thank you!

For more information about Packt, please visit `packt.com`.

Section 1: Introduction to Software Quality Assurance

We are going to learn about the thought process behind software quality assurance and the quality management standards used in the industry. Then, we will familiarize ourselves with the software development process and its phases. We will also learn about managing the deliverables that are generated at each stage of the software development life cycle.

This section will include the following chapter:

- Chapter 1, *An Overview of Software Quality Assurance*

1
An Overview of Software Quality Assurance

Do we, as human beings, make mistakes? The answer to that is an overwhelming *yes*. There are examples of failures in quality control and decision-making that have shaken the world and resulted in huge losses to the companies involved. For example, we all remember the tragic accident with the Challenger space shuttle that exploded on launch. Was this a case of simple oversight or was it possible to have adequately tested the systems to control the threat of failure and avoid the explosion?

To get to the bottom of such incidents, we need to learn from the very people who are involved in the design and production of such systems. Mistakes are generally unavoidable and can happen at any stage of production, due to reasons such as weak or unclear requirements, hurrying to meet deadlines, or insufficient knowledge about a system. What we can do, however, is follow a process that can help reduce making or introducing any new errors, while preventing known errors from being repeated. This calls for a change in thought processes and a reliance on crafting standard practices in order to produce more successful products. Let's first understand what quality means before we embark on our journey to rewire ourselves to create sustainable and repeatable best practices for delivering defect-free software.

In this chapter, we'll be covering the following topics:

- What is quality?
- How do we ensure quality?
- Software testing thought process
- Quality Management Systems
- Software Development Life Cycle versus Software Testing Life Cycle
- Types of testing
- Preparing test data and managing test artifacts

What is quality?

Quality, just like any other measure, requires a frame of reference or standards for us to compare against customer needs. These standards can help us to maintain and promote the consistency of the products developed, minimize the amount of rework required, and produce a customer-oriented product.

Quality can be defined in different ways. According to the **International Organization for Standardization (ISO)** 13628-2:2006, quality can be defined as conformance to specified requirements.

There are seven main ISO principles (by ISO 9000) that revolve around making a good quality product:

- Customer focus
- Leadership
- Engagement of people
- Process approach
- Improvement
- Evidence-based decision-making
- Relationship management

The quality model presented by ISO (ISO/IEC 25010:2011) is useful to assess the quality of products. Adoption of this model can guide organizations on how to improve the quality of software. This model describes the quality characteristics and sub-characteristics that software should possess to qualify as production-ready before it can be released to end users. Let's take a closer look at these characteristics and sub-characteristics.

The product quality model relates to the static properties of software and the dynamic properties of a computer system:

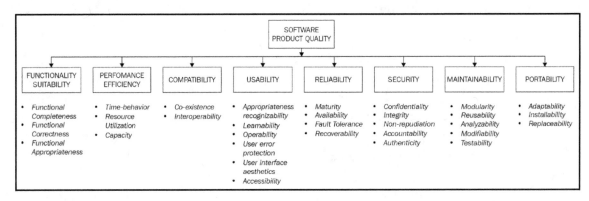

As you can see in the preceding diagram, there are eight product quality characteristics, which I will explain to you:

- **FUNCTIONAL SUITABILITY:** Characterizes the functional potential and abilities of the software by sub-categorizing it into three different categories:
    - **Completeness**: The measurement of the set of functions implemented and covered for all the specified requirements to satisfy user goals
    - **Correctness**: The measurement of deviation from the specified requirements and the measurement of the precision of the generation of end results
    - **Appropriateness**: The measurement of the generation of suitable and relevant results that can facilitate achieving specified tasks and objectives
- **PERFORMANCE EFFICIENCY**: Takes three main factors into consideration:
    - **Time-behavior**: Measures the response times, processing times, and tolerance of the throughput of an application against the specified load
    - **Resource utilization**: A measurement of the utilization of the amount and types of resources while performing specified tasks
    - **Capacity**: Checks maximum tolerance and limitations to meeting the required goal
- **COMPATIBILITY**: This checks whether the system can work efficiently in different environments by examining the following two factors:
    - **Co-existence:** Verifies that software or a product can perform its tasks effectively by sharing common resources and environments with other software/hardware
    - **Interoperability**: Ensures the exchange of information between two separate products or components is smooth and has no impact on the intended results
- **USABILITY:** Examines the ease of use of software by considering the following aspects:
    - **Appropriateness recognizability**: The verification of the product or service against the user's needs
    - **Learnability**: The extent to which a product or service facilitates users' learning of its usage effectively and efficiently
    - **Operability:** Deals with knowing how easy it is to operate, control, and use the system product or service effectively

- **User error protection**: Measures the degree to which the system can prevent users from making errors
- **User interface aesthetics**: Checks how the user interface of the system can yield user satisfaction and a pleasing experience
- **Accessibility**: Makes sure that users can use the system hassle-free, so that users can use it effectively, without compromising its ability to perform a specified set of goals or the purpose that has been set for the system or products

- **RELIABILITY:** The extent to which end users can rely on the system or products to perform specific tasks or activities. It consists of four sub-categories:
  - **Maturity:** The extent to which the system or its components meets customers' needs in terms of reliability when functioning normally
  - **Availability:** The measurement of the availability and accessibility of the software or product whenever users want to use it
  - **Fault-tolerance:** The measurement of the deviation of the expected results despite being under undesirable conditions
  - **Recoverability:** Checks how quickly the system can recover from interruptions or failures without losing information
- **SECURITY:** Everyone wants their data to be secure when it comes to using software products or services. Security is needed to control the unauthorized use of data. In order to meet security needs, it has been sub-categorized into the following categories:
  - **Confidentiality**: Ensures the authorized use of data
  - **Integrity**: Capability to prevent unauthorized and unofficial access to data by invalid users, products, or other services that could potentially cause harm by modifying data
  - **Non-repudiation**: Refers to the degree to which the actions and/or events can be ascertained to have occurred so that it cannot be disputed or repudiated late
  - **Accountability**: Ensures that activities or actions performed by an actor in the system can be traced back uniquely to having been performed by the same actor
  - **Authenticity:** Ensures that the actor or person is uniquely identifiable in the system, which can be proven to match the identity as claimed

- **MAINTAINABILITY:** Deals with the maintenance of the software product or service to fulfill customer needs and to continue to perform efficiently. It has been sub-categorized into the following:
    - **Modularity**: Measures the effect on the other parts or components of the system when one part undergoes a change. High cohesion and low coupling are what we strive to achieve. Thus, the code for a particular module should be closely related within the module but each module should function independently from other modules.
    - **Reusability**: Refers to the degree to which specific parts or components of software can be reused.
    - **Analyzability**: Deals with checking the ease of analyzing the software or product in order to detect failures, deficiencies, and/or the impact of modifications.
    - **Modifiability**: A measurement of the extent to which the software product or service is modifiable without affecting its current efficiency and functionality.
    - **Testability**: Defines the baseline for the test that confirms whether the software product or service meets the specified requirements.

- **PORTABILITY:** Defines the resilience of the system to perform efficiently with the changes in software, hardware, or the environment.
    - **Adaptability**: A measurement of the extent to which the software system or product can be adopted without affecting its efficiency
    - **Installability**: A measurement of the capacity of a product or software to be installed or uninstalled in a stipulated environment
    - **Replaceability**: The ability of software to be replaced with other software to perform the same set of tasks in the same environment

The **QUALITY IN USE** model is applicable to the complete human-computer interaction and has the following five characteristics:

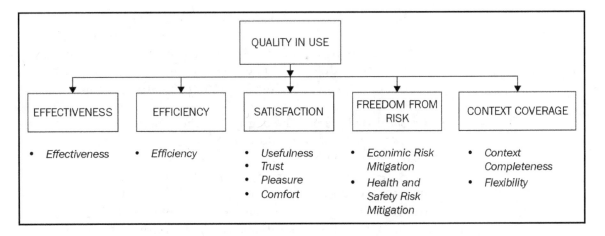

Let's look at these characteristics in detail:

- **EFFECTIVENESS:** A measure of the accuracy and completeness of results generated by the component or functions of the software product or service.
- **EFFICIENCY:** A measurement of the utilization of resources needed to produce complete and accurate results.
- **SATISFACTION**: These are four ways to test user satisfaction with software:
    - **Usefulness:** Makes sure that the software satisfies customer needs and functions as expected
    - **Trust**: Ensures software fulfills customer expectations
    - **Pleasure**: A measurement of how much the software product or service helps customers meet their needs
    - **Comfort**: The degree to which the user is satisfied with the software product and feels comfortable using it
- **FREEDOM FROM RISK**: There are three main ways to analyze the level to which a system can reduce potential risks, as follows:
    - **Economic Risk Mitigation**: Analyzes how much the system can mitigate potential risks that could have a severe impact on various levels, such as financial, commercial, reputation, and disrupt the efficiency of the software product or service
    - **Health and Safety Risk Mitigation**: Identifies the level to which software can mitigate potential risks to end users

- **Environmental Risk Mitigation**: Identifies how much software can mitigate the potential risk to property or the environment
- **CONTEXT COVERAGE:** The level to which the system meets the specified context can be measured by the following:
  - **Context Completeness**: Verifies that software meets specified objectives and can be used efficiently without any risk in all specified contexts of use
  - **Flexibility**: A measurement of the degree to which the software can be used beyond the specified requirements

These characteristics can help us to assess a software product's quality.

Why should you care about quality?

It takes a lot of work to establish a brand and even more work to continue to build it and to sustain trust in the brand. To survive in today's competitive market and to maintain a good reputation, organizations incorporate testing phases and dedicate time to testing and debugging software products in the Software Development Life Cycle. Building quality products reduces the risk involved and boosts performance. A well-designed product can decrease the level of user dissatisfaction and frustration. It also increases the product's reliability and improves the end user's experience, resulting in happy customers.

Who is responsible for quality?

Products and services have a direct impact on their customer base, since they are released on the market to solve a problem that customers face. Thus, it is imperative that organizations that provide such services or products are responsible for their quality both before and after they hit the market. Organizations need to consider both internal and external environmental factors that can affect a product. This requires proper planning and delegation to dedicate teams and resources to each facet of the product. Usually, teams consist of the following roles:

- Product managers
- Project managers
- **Quality Assurance (QA)** managers
- Business analysts
- Software developers
- QA engineers/testers

This team works toward the defined goal together and delivers the product. There are other focus areas in which we need to perform some groundwork to help organizations effectively manage the delivery of quality products, but the focus should always be on improving products and services. Knowing your customer is the first step in enhancing the quality and standards of the products or services they receive. Sustaining them is the key to a successful product. In the next section, we will discuss the process of developing sustainable, high-quality products and services.

How do we ensure quality?

Quality assurance is the key to the success of any business. The software development process goes through various phases, and ensuring quality at every step is a must. In the previous section, we saw why it's important to deliver a quality product. In this section, we'll learn how we can deliver quality products.

Delivering a project with a defined scope within a specified amount of time, with a set budget, and with certain quality standards expected by the customer are key factors in making a project successful. However, reaching a reasonable trade-off between these factors is necessary to get to market quickly and to remain competitive.

For example, if the scope of the project increases while the resources and time remain the same, it will affect quality directly, since the team to remain to deliver more within the stipulated time frame. Since their work hours do not change, the team might have to cut the testing time or reduce test coverage to deliver on time. The following diagram depicts the Iron Triangle:

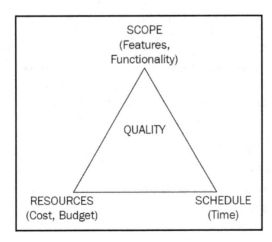

The Iron Triangle

The objectives of the triangle—also referred to as the Iron Triangle—help us to deliver projects successfully. To ensure quality, we need to satisfy the Iron Triangle's objectives. A traditional project management triangle consists of the following:

SCOPE	• Ensuring that we have verified and confirmed the scope of the project with the customer and excluded what is out of the scope of the project • Ensuring that we have designed a requirement specification document and all supporting documents that are required for the completion of the project • Ensuring that we have identified all sets of test cases and scenarios to validate the scope as specified in the requirement document and test plan
Time	• Ensuring that all activities and their dependent activities are planned appropriately • Ensuring that activities also constitute meeting time, sanctioned holidays, resource availability, and buffer time as part of the contingency plan • Ensuring that every project kickoff occurs on time
Cost	• Ensuring that all resources based on skill set and budget have been identified for the project • Ensuring that all the required tools, vendor products, and purchasing licenses have been either acquired or renewed to fit the specified budget
QUALITY	• Ensuring that test managers and test leaders have done a requirement-gap analysis and are ready with a test plan • Ensuring that the test plan lists all of the factors that might affect the quality of the software product, such as resources, their skill level, the tools required, things within scope, things out of scope, testing strategies, test methodologies, compatibility, and supported browsers versions

The Iron Triangle helps project managers to analyze and understand the trade-offs while catering to these factors. A proper balance must be achieved to ensure the desired levels of quality to produce a successful product.

Software testing thought process

Software products are the result of a multidisciplinary team coming together to make a concrete product that serves customer needs. Although the team is formed of several roles, such as managers, analysts, developers, and testers, each role is essential to deliver a suitable and robust product. This requires each of these contributors to be a part of the quality process.

If every role has a part in ensuring quality, why do we need a separate role for testers? One simple reason is to introduce a fresh set of eyes. While it is possible for a developer to test their own code or software, it requires a different mindset to ensure quality. A developer's mindset is to prove that their software works, but a tester's mindset is to make the product fail to work. Thus, the tester's role is more about finding defects in the software.

Now that we understand the difference in the thought process required for software testing, let's discuss the key skills an effective tester should possess:

- **Analytical thinking**: There are various methods to approach a problem, however, solutions based on the analysis of data tend to be more accurate and optimal. Hence, a tester should analyze complex problems first and then design steps to resolve it. It helps a tester to plan and come up with various scenarios to compare with the business requirements.

- **Observability**: Good observational skills and attention to detail are always important when trying to identify defects. This makes our job easy by simply observing and identifying what's not working. This helps testers to design end-to-end workflows, comparing the throughput, validating UI design and functionality, and so on.

- **Logical thinking**: Pattern analysis is another aspect of noticing what is going wrong and where the problem could lie – recognizing patterns, connecting the dots, and the ability to perform root-cause analysis are things that help testers stay relevant in the event of automation.

- **Reasoning**: It's always better to know an application in depth, not only its functionalities and user interface but also the logic built in the code. Supporting your reasoning with artifacts or proof is essential. Artifacts, such as logs and screenshots, are good sources of proof that testers can provide along with a defect. Not only does this help to reproduce defects, it also helps developers to debug code and provides a place to start debugging.

- **Test-to-break attitude**: You should have a mindset that is bent on breaking the application. In order to do that, you need to first understand how the specific function or application being tested works. This results in generating ideas for scenarios that can help to find hidden and latent defects.

- **Broadening perspective**: Domain knowledge adds value when it comes to verifying a product, as, sometimes, it's essential for testers to think from a broader perspective. Testing is not limited to verifying the part or component of the software where the changes have been made; it also deals with testing the parts where nothing has changed. Verifying whether the developed product works in a different environment, with different software, and whole different set of parameters, makes it more reliable.

- **Understanding end user's perspective**: Testing is not always about breaking; it's also about ensuring that the software works as expected and satisfies the intended purpose. Hence, when validating software, testing from an end user's perspective helps testers see different dimensions to perform verification effectively.

- **Good communication skills**: This plays a key role in team environments—it helps testers collaborate better and build a rapport as a team. Testers play a very delicate role, which is to effectively find flaws in developers' code. Hence, it is imperative for them to ensure the team focuses collectively to improve the software rather than blaming the developers.
- **Thinking outside the box**: Out-of-the-box thinking results in finding pathways that have probably not been explored before. This helps testers to find hidden and not-so-obvious defects.
- **Learning attitude**: As technology keeps changing, it is a must for a tester to keep themselves abreast with the newest technology. Learning new skills is crucial for them to be able to survive and adapt.

Quality Management Systems

As we have seen so far, there are various ways we can ensure quality in our projects, but how do we evaluate whether the quality system we pick is effective? This becomes more of a concern if one organization needs to contract its work to another and needs to know whether the contractor will be able to provide quality services and products. This need for the quality system to be auditable necessitates the use of a **Quality Management System (QMS)**.

A QMS is a set of standards that defines how an organization can meet the requirements of its customers and other stakeholders. Quality standards are a set of guidelines, rather than actual standards, that have been widely accepted in the software industry with defined processes and evaluation metrics to help improve the quality of software. The motivation for the selection of a standard is left to the business and the management to decide. Once certified, it is imperative to have the quality plan in place based on the certification that is opted for.

All quality standards have the same underlying principles:

- Well-defined processes to develop software
- Aligning people with processes to synergize and promote commitment to the quality-improvement program
- Enforcing the requirement to produce documentation for each process

Thus, processes should be used as facilitators for quality improvement rather than a hindrance. It is the management's responsibility to foster a culture within the organization that works within the well-defined framework for development while promoting incentives to drive quality at every step of the development process.

There are several software-engineering standards that have been developed by major standardization and certification bodies. The ISO 9000 and **Capability Maturity Model Integration (CMMI)** are the most widely-used international standards in software-engineering and product-development organizations. Let's look at them in detail to understand how implementing standards can help an organization to ensure quality.

ISO 9000 series

ISO 9000 is a set of standards defined by ISO. If an organization needed to be certified, it would certify for the latest standard, ISO 9001:2015, which replaced the previous version, ISO 9001:2008. ISO 9001:2015 provides guidelines that drive continual improvement for an organization.

This latest update is based on the **High-Level Structure (HLS)**—Annex SL, which helps organizations incorporate more than one management system into core business processes and make efficiencies.

The ISO 9001:2015 standard specifies 10 clauses, as summarized in the following points:

- **Clause 1 (Scope)**: Explains what the standard is for and what it encompasses. The scope clause covers the following aspects:
    - The goals and objectives of the standard to understand the expectations of the certifying organization
    - The approach and reference to customer requirements
    - The approach and reference to regulatory or statutory requirements
    - The applicability of the standard requirements, since they are applicable to all sorts of organizations, regardless of their type, size, or the products and services being provided
- **Clause 2 (Normative references)**: Includes the terms, principles, fundamental concepts, and vocabulary that are essential for the application of the ISO 9001 standard. It also provides references to other documentation to assist in complying with the requirements of the ISO 9001 standard.
- **Clause 3 (Terms and definitions)**: Specifies the terms and definitions given in the ISO 9000:2015 that apply to ISO 9001. This clause helps to clarify unfamiliar terms and resolves unnecessary disputes or conflicts.

- **Clause 4 (Context of the organization)**: Establishes the context of the QMS. The organization achieves this by doing the following:
  - Identifying relevant external—such as market-driven, local or global environments, and competition—and internal factors—such as values, culture, or the performance of the organization—that can affect the quality of the product being delivered.
  - Establishing the requirements and expectations of all stakeholders.
  - Determining the scope of the QMS; whether it needs to be implemented organization-wide or for relevant business functions.
  - Establishing, maintaining, and continually improving the QMS using a process approach.

- **Clause 5 (Leadership)**: Dictates the activities required from top management for the success of a QMS, as follows:
  - Being actively engaged in the operation of the QMS and ensuring that it is embedded in the organization's processes
  - Direct and establish a quality policy that aligns with the business strategy to formalize the goals and commitment required from all parties
  - Ensure that roles, responsibilities, and authorities are defined for all employees and that everyone involved is made aware of them

- **Clause 6 (Planning)**: Focuses on creating an action plan to address risks and opportunities. It requires the organization to do the following:
  - Understand the risks and opportunities relevant to the scope of the organization, as required in clause 4
  - Establish clear, measurable, and documented quality objectives with an action plan to monitor, control, and communicate risks and opportunities effectively
  - Create a change-management plan to carry out changes to the system in a systematic way

- **Clause 7 (Support)**: Stresses the basic HLS clauses of bringing the right resources, the right people, and the right infrastructure, are as follows:
  - Ensure adequate resources are provisioned, which includes employees, equipment, and IT systems
  - Assess existing competence and fill gaps in competence with training and documentation
  - Awareness about the quality policy is a must for all personnel, as there is also the need to understand the relevance of their roles and the implications of non-conformance

- Communication, both external and internal, is key to the success of the system; the organization needs to plan and implement an effective communication process
- Document information to demonstrate compliance in any format that suits the organization while implementing appropriate access controls for information security
- **Clause 8 (Operation)**: Focuses on enabling the organization to meet customer requirements by executing plans and processes, as follows:
  - Establish appropriate performance monitoring for the continual improvement of all functions
  - Understand customer requirements for products and services through effective communication
  - Create a design plan that includes all customer specifications, budget, drawings, and so on
  - Require the organization to select, evaluate, and re-evaluate all external entities sourced for procuring processes, products, or services
  - Clarity in product specification and evaluation to monitor whether the processes, products, or services being provided by the external entity conform to the customer's requirements
  - The need for systematic planning and the execution of all production operations to ensure quality control and to demonstrate the capabilities to deliver consistently to meet customer expectations
  - Monitor and measure products and/or services to verify conformance to customer requirements, and have the evidence duly documented by authorized personnel before the product or service is released to the customer
  - The control of nonconforming output being released to the customer and the establishment of a course of action to handle nonconforming deliveries
- **Clause 9 (Performance Evaluation)**: Details ways to measure and evaluate the QMS to ensure it is effective and sustainable:
  - Utilize simple analysis methods, such as bar charts, or complex statistical process controls to analyze collected data to identify opportunities for improvement and to measure the effectiveness of the management system

- Establish a clear and consistent internal audit program to audit processes at regular frequencies to find nonconformities and trigger preventive measures for improvement
- Require top management to be involved in reviewing the quality-management system to ensure continuing suitability, adequacy, and effectiveness

- **Clause 10 (Improvement)**: Requires the organization to determine and identify what improvement means with regard to the following cases:
    - Establish means of improvement by reviewing processes, products, or services, and analyzing the results from the management system
    - Begin corrective actions to prevent the recurrence of non-conformities by using root-cause analysis, problem-solving methods, and providing training to improve capabilities
    - Build a feedback mechanism that requires the management system to utilize input such as corrective actions, internal audits, management reviews, and customer feedback for continual improvement

These clauses can be grouped in relation to **Plan-Do-Check-Act (PDCA)**, since it is the operating principle of the ISO 9001 process approach, which drives continuous improvement in the organization. The PDCA principle combines planning, implementing, controlling, and improving the operations of a QMS, as shown in the following diagram:

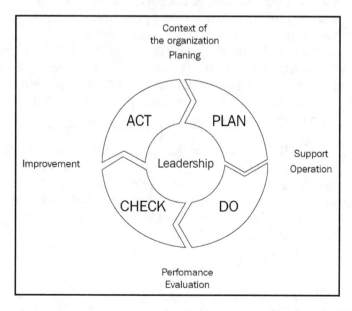

Let's look at each stage of the PDCA cycle:

PLAN	In the planning stage, top management provides engagement in understanding the context of the organization by identifying factors affecting quality, establishing customer expectations, and defining the scope of the QMS (clause 4). Top management then commits to establishing a quality policy (clause 5) and an action plan to address the risks and opportunities relevant to the scope. The plan needs to be clear and precise so that executing the plan is easy (clause 6). Finally, support structures are identified and implemented to carry out the plan (clause 7).
DO	In the Do phase, the organization executes the plans and processes, developing and releasing products or services to meet customer requirements. This requires us to identify relevant controls, be clear in our understanding of product specifications, and monitor and control the product's release to weed out any non-conformities (clause 8).
CHECK	In this stage, management assesses the effectiveness of the execution of the plan by monitoring, measuring, analyzing, and evaluating the performance and effectiveness of the quality-management system using internal audits and management reviews. Additionally, we use simple methods of analysis or complex statistical-process controls to identify opportunities for improvement (clause 9).
ACT	In this stage, the team *acts* to address issues that were discovered in the Check stage to improve the performance of the plan. This stage requires the application of the principles of leadership and commitment discussed in Clause 5 of the standard, such as taking accountability for the effectiveness of the QMS, and engaging, directing, and supporting people to contribute to the effectiveness of the QMS. We also identify opportunities for improvement, evaluate non-conformities, perform corrective actions, and create a feedback loop for continuous improvement (clause 10).

Here's an example of the PDCA cycle for an SQA team—if the team wanted to increase the number of defects detected in each release sprint by 20%, the team would create a plan for making changes to the processes, following which the changes would be made to the process, and the process would be executed. After execution, checking the results shows a defect detection ratio of 15%, which is then acted on to make further changes. This is then taken up in the next planning phase to plan defect-detection until the goal of 20% is reached.

CMMI

CMMI is a set of guidelines that enable organizations to produce good-quality software and improve its performance. CMMI was developed mainly to assess an organization's ability to take on large development projects for the US Department of Defense.

CMMI released version 2 of the model in March 2018. This was an update from version 1.3. CMMI v2.0 is divided into 4 categories and 10 capabilities with 25 practice areas.

Now let's understand the categories and the practice areas:

- **Doing**: This category deals with designing and developing high-quality products that adhere to customer needs while reducing supply-chain risks. The doing stage includes four capabilities with 10 practice areas, as follows:
    - **Ensuring quality (ENQ)**:
        - **Developing and managing requirements**: Obtaining requirements, ensuring the mutual understanding of stakeholders, and aligning requirements, plans, and work products.
        - **Process quality assurance**: Verifying and enabling the improvement of the quality of the processes performed and the resulting products.
        - **Verification and validation**: Processes for this practice area should do the following:
            - Verify that the selected solutions and components meet their requirements
            - Validate that the selected solutions and components fulfill their intended use in their target environments
        - **Peer review**: Utilize **subject matter experts (SMEs)** and peers to review the product to identify and address issues.
    - **Engineering and Developing Products (EDP)**:
        - **Product integration**: Integrating and delivering a quality solution that meets the required functionality
        - **Technical solution**: Designing and building solutions that meet customer requirements

- **Delivering and Managing Services (DMS)**:
    - **Service delivery management**: Delivering products and services while conforming to **service-level agreements (SLAs)**
    - **Strategic service management**: Establishing and maintaining data regarding the organization's capabilities and strategic needs, which serve as standard services

- **Selecting and Managing Suppliers (SMS)**:
    - **Supplier source selection**: Selecting a supplier by evaluating whether the supplier-delivered solution meets the expected requirements
    - **Supplier agreement management**: Establishing an agreement with the selected suppliers and ensuring that the terms are adhered to by both supplier and acquirer

- **Managing**: This category deals with improving staff productivity while managing disruptions from the Porter's Five Forces model to achieve speed-to-market. This category includes three capabilities with seven practice areas, as follows:
    - **Planning and Managing Work (PMW)**:
        - **Estimating**: Forecasting the factors of the Iron Triangle needed to produce quality product or solution.
        - **Planning**: Developing plans describing delivery processes based on the standards and constraints of the organization. This includes budget, schedule, and resources, as well as stakeholders and the development team.
        - **Monitor and Control**: Tracking the project's progress to assert appropriate controls if the project deviates from the plan.
    - **Managing Business Resilience (MBR)**:
        - **Risk management and opportunity management**: Identifying, recording, and managing potential risks and opportunities

- **Incident resolution and prevention**: Analyzing nonconformance to find the root cause and create a plan to prevent the event from recurring
- **Continuity**: Establishing contingency plans for sustaining operations during emergencies

- **Managing the Workforce** (**MWF**):
    - **Organizational training**: Developing the skills and knowledge of personnel so that they perform their roles efficiently and effectively

- **Enabling**: This category deals with securing stakeholder buy-in and assuring product integrity. It includes one capability with three practice areas, as follows:
    - **Supporting Implementation** (**SI**):
        - **Causal analysis and resolution**: Understanding the root cause of all results and acting to prevent the recurrence of nonconformities and/or acting to ensure conformities
        - **Decision analysis and resolution**: Making and recording decisions using a recorded process that analyzes alternatives
        - **Configuration management**: Managing the integrity of deliveries using version control, change control, and appropriate audit mechanisms

- **Improving**: This category deals with ensuring that performance goals support business needs while establishing sustainable efficiencies. It includes two capabilities and five practice areas, as follows:
    - **Improving Performance** (**IMP**):
        - **Process management**: Managing and implementing the continuous improvement of processes and infrastructure to identify the most beneficial process improvements that support accomplishing business objectives in a sustainable way
        - **Process asset development**: Recording and maintaining the list of processes used to perform the work
        - **Managing performance and measurement**: Managing performance using measurement and analysis to achieve business objectives

- **Sustaining Habit and Persistence (SHP)**:
  - **Governance**: Counselling top management in the sponsorship and governance of process activities
  - **Implementation infrastructure**: Ensuring that processes important to the organization are continuously used and improved

 To learn more and get updates about the new CMMI v2.0, please visit `https://www.cmmiinstitute.com/cmmi/model-viewer`.

Maturity levels

The previously-mentioned categories and process areas are basically factors to improve the business performance of an organization. The ranks at which these organizations would be at, based on how they have implemented those process areas, are called **maturity levels**.

The following diagram shows the levels of software-process maturity. Based on software-process maturity, an organization can be at one of these six maturity levels:

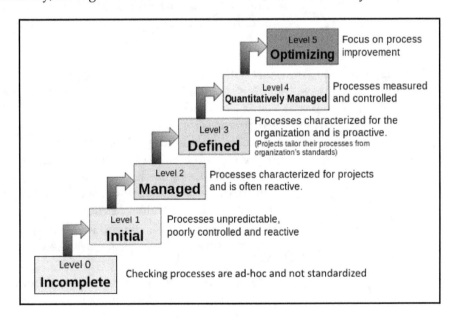

https://commons.wikimedia.org/wiki/File:Characteristics_of_Capability_Maturity_Model.svg

Let's look at these maturity levels in detail:

- **Maturity Level 0 (Incomplete)**: Organizations at this level do not have any defined processes. These organizations usually work on ad hoc procedures, and any positive outcomes are the result of chance. Work in these organizations may or may not get completed.
- **Maturity Level 1 (Initial)**: Organizations at this level are characterized by last-minute chaos in terms of delivery due to a lack of clarity. Work in these organizations gets completed but its success is dependent on one or a few highly competent people. In most cases, work is often delayed and over-budget.
- **Maturity Level 2 (Managed)**: Organizations at this level follow a well-defined process at the project level. Every project is planned and executed in a systematic way. Every activity is measured and controlled to be managed and improved upon later.
- **Maturity Level 3 (Defined)**: Organizations at this level have a well-defined process across the organization, and processes at the project level are derived from ones defined at the organizational level. These organizations have clearer definitions of processes compared to Level 2 organizations, and targets to achieve performance objectives at both the project and organization levels. Efforts are also made to measure and continuously improve process definitions.
- **Maturity Level 4 (Quantitatively Managed)**: Organizations at this level build on Level 3 practices, and use statistical and other quantitative techniques to understand process performance and product quality. Utilizing scientific quantitative tools helps the organization identify and predict variations, which provides agility to improve and achieve quality and performance objectives.
- **Maturity Level 5 (Optimizing)**: Organizations at Level 5 build on Level 4 practices and utilize quantitative techniques to continuously optimize their process and product performance. These organizations are flexible and able to pivot, thus providing a platform for agility and innovation.

I hope the introduction to QMS has sparked an interest in understanding and learning more about the management systems in place in your current organization.

 To learn more about maturity levels and the adoption of the CMMI in your organization, make sure to check out `https://consulting.itgonline.com/cmmi-consulting/cmmi-v2/`.

There are various ways in which continuous improvement can be achieved in either CMMI or ISO 9001:2015 implementations. You can also integrate business improvement processes, such as Six Sigma quality control or the **Consortium for IT software Quality** (**CISQ**) quality model. A clear understanding of business processes, and alignment with the company goals and objectives are necessary for the success of the system.

Software Development Life Cycle versus Software Testing Life Cycle

The **Software Development Life Cycle** (**SDLC**) is a process to develop and deliver software products or services that details the end-to-end phase, from designing, coding, and testing, to maintaining the product after release. The **Software Testing Life Cycle** (**STLC**) is a subset of the SDLC. Let's explore both the SDLC and STLC in detail.

SDLC

The SDLC is a planned and organized process that divides software development tasks into various phases. These phases help the team to build a product that adheres to the factors of scope, time, cost, and quality. It also helps the project manager to monitor and control project activities at each stage and perform risk analysis effectively.

Any traditional SDLC comprises the following basic, but critical, phases:

- **Requirement analysis:** A software product exists to solve a problem for the customer. Understanding customer needs is hence essential to building one. Requirement analysis is the phase where this is achieved. This is the stage where we try to answer the question, *what do we want to build and why?*
    - We create formal documentation (for example, a **Business Requirement Document** (**BRD**)) with customer needs, wants, and wish lists.
    - We also identify the objectives, goals, risks, resources, and the technology being used, as well as its limitations.
    - We need to specify what is within and what is out of scope for the selected iteration or version of the software that has been committed to for the customer. Usually, a team of client managers, business analysts, and project managers work together to prepare the final version of the business requirement document. Once it's ready and approved, the team moves on to the designing phase.

- **Designing:** Designing is done based on the requirement documents.
    - In this phase, the team prepares high-level and low-level design documents, to further narrow down the broad requirements
    - These documents help to establish a logical relationship between different components of the application, and define its architecture in detail, including a format, look and feel, and a UI mockup
    - Once everything is ready, it moves on to the team of developers to start with actual coding
- **Coding:** The end of the designing phase kicks off the start of the coding phase, where developers start to build actual applications.
    - In this phase, developers convert every component, the logical relationships between them, and build the architecture as mentioned in the high-level and low-level documents. The main goal here is to generate an actual workable software product or service, as designed in the mockup.
    - Developers make sure to meet the customer requirements mentioned in the requirement documents.
    - Developers also perform unit testing, a method for testing functions to get the desired results by passing different input parameters.
    - Once the code looks good and it's ready for the testers to verify, the developers deploy it in the test environment and make it available for the testers to start testing.
- **Testing:** This is where testers verify the application to confirm that it meets customer requirements. The main goal is to determine whether the solution works for customer needs without any issues or defects.
    - As a part of the testing process, testers verify critical paths, verify all the necessary workflows, and perform happy path testing. However, they also try to break the application by passing invalid parameters in the form of negative testing.
    - Using different testing types, they confirm whether the product or service is acceptable to the user, and think from the end user's perspective when validating every single text field, checkbox, links, and buttons—in short, every single UI component of the application.

- Testing the application under stress to see how it reacts under extreme conditions and how it performs by adding load to it are parts of performance testing. Once the software is thoroughly tested and confirmed, with the number of known defects, which are either in closed or deferred status, it's shipped to the end users.

- **Maintenance:** This is where errors get reported or suggestions and/or enhancements get added by end users after realizing the product or service are implemented, as a part of the maintenance phase. It can also be a part of releasing or upgrading the current version of the software or service.
    - A dedicated team works on this phase, where team members interact with their clients or end users to get feedback, issues, or errors
    - They also provide documents to help customers learn how to use a software product or service, efficiently

STLC

The STLC is part of the SDLC. It's a systematic approach that ensures the quality of a software product or services. Like the SDLC, the STLC also consists of different phases, listed as follows:

- **Requirement analysis:** Once the project gets initiated, the team actively starts working on gathering customer requirements. In this phase, testers, business analysts, and developers take a closer look at each specification requested by users. For requirement analysis in STLC, testers can do the following things:
    - Testers need to break drown broader and more complex requirements into smaller pieces to understand the testable requirements, the scope of the testing, and verification key points, and to identify the gaps in the requirements
    - They can clarify their doubts regarding technology or software requirements, limitations and dependencies, and so on with the developers and business analysts, and improve suggestions or highlight missing information that needs to be added into the requirements
    - Testers can also highlight risks and develop risk-mitigation strategies before proceeding to the test-planning phase

- **Test planning:** This is where testers (usually lead testers or managers) plan testing activities and milestones based on various factors, such as time, scope, and resources that help them to track the progress of the project. Let's check out some activities that the tester performs during test planning:
    - In this phase, testers plan test activities and strategies that can be used effectively during the subsequent testing phases
    - Also, the scope of testing needs to be identified and parts out of scope should be marked as well
    - They also need to decide on the testing techniques and types that will be implemented during the test-execution phase based on the current product requirements
    - Along with that, an understanding of the tool's requirements and the number of resources required with their skill level can help them plan tasks better

    Considering these factors and the timelines for the selected project, a tester can prepare an effective test plan that will fit into the project budget and help the team to create a quality product.

- **Test designing:** This is where the test team starts to break down each requirement and converts them into test scenarios. These test scenarios cover happy path, positive testing, the critical path that needs to be verified, and functions that need to be verified with a different set of parameters. It also consists of negatives scenarios, acceptance tests, and scenarios based on user-interaction workflows and data flows.
    - Based on the type of application and the types of testing listed in the requirement analysis, phase testers can work on creating automated test scripts, adding scenarios for stress and load testing, and performance testing can help testers to test the application better and find more defects.
    - Once the scenarios are ready and reviewed, testers move on to preparing the test cases or test scripts (in the case of automation testing) in order to list the detailed steps.
    - One scenario can have one or more test cases, whereas a requirement can be linked to one or more scenarios. This mapping is helpful when creating a **Requirement Traceability Matrix (RTM)**.

- **Environment setup:** Establishing a separate test environment is always good practice. Keeping testing code distinct from development code can help both testers and developers debug the code in the specific version and get to the root cause more quickly. Also, it gives developers a chance to make bug fixes in the code and in their copy of the code, and to verify it in their environment to confirm that the fix is working before sending it to the testers. It saves the time and effort needed to log defects and collect artifacts.
  - When setting up the environment, testers need to ensure that they have configured the required version of the tool, the software, the hardware, and the test data.
  - They also need to make sure that they have authorization to access the environment with the required roles to test the application, databases, and other tools required. The testing environment should mimic the end user's environment. This results in documenting the known behavior of the product and helps to manage expectations after delivery.
- **Test execution:** Once the code is ready and unit tested by the developers, it's deployed in the test environment so that testers can initiate the test-execution phase.
  - The first test that testers perform is a smoke test to validate whether the software product or service caters to the basic requirements
  - After the software passes the smoke test, testers can continue with the validation process, following the types of testing as planned during the test-planning phase
  - During the execution phase, testers log an undesirable result as a defect. Once the defects have been fixed, testers need to retest the parts that have been changed and the part of the application that has not been changed, as part of regression testing

- **Test reporting:** It is very important for testers, leads, and managers to track and monitor the progress of the project consistently so that it becomes easy to identify obstacles or risks early. It also helps being agile to provide the solution and resolve the problem.
    - Reporting the test helps the stakeholders to know the status of the test execution after each iteration or test cycle.
    - It also helps defect managers to identify the blocked test case that is dependent on the defect.
    - Accordingly, its priority or severity can be changed so that it can help to progress test execution.
    - At the end of all iterations, a final report is prepared with the number of defects found during the test execution phase, the number of defects closed or marked as deferred, and the number of test cases passed or marked **N/A**. Along with this report, all the artifacts are validated and made sure that it's been added whenever it's needed.

- **Closure:** During the closure phase, test managers or test leads make sure that all the tests completed successfully, as per the schedule.
    - Team leads or managers make sure that all the required deliverables and closure documents are approved and accepted as per the evaluation criteria, and signed off as part of the closure phase

We will be learning more about each phase in the STLC, along with its practical implementation in Jira and using its plugin, in the following chapters.

Types of testing

To ensure the quality of the product, we need to understand our application and its testing needs to make it more robust and bug-free. Based on the customer requirements and the type of product we are developing, we can come up with a list of the types of testing that are needed during the test planning phase of STLC.

In this section, we will be learning about the different testing types that can be used during the test-execution phase:

- **Black-box testing:** Pays attention to external behavior, specifications, and desirable end results produced by the application by passing a set of known input parameters rather than the internal structure of the code. The main goal here is to verify the software in the way the end user will test or use it without having knowledge of the internal workings of the system under test. Black box testing helps testers to identify whether it meets all stated and unstated requirements and behaves as per end user's perspective. There are various techniques that can be used in this testing type:

  - **Analysis of requirements specification**: Confirms whether the software behaves as specified in the requirement specification document. It is reachable and available for end users to use, it behaves consistently and accurately. Testers prepares traceability matrix, where they confirm that their test scenarios have covered all the stated requirements. We will be covering requirement traceability in detail in the following chapters.

  - **Positive testing and negative testing**: Positive testing refers to validating all the positive scenarios, in short, happy path testing. It verifies whether the end-to-end workflows, or part of the workflows, function as expected. Negative testing is the reverse of positive testing, where the intent is to show that the application does not behave as expected. In this case, testers must come with a set of input parameters, or conditions in which the application will not withstand and break. This is a very effective way to find loopholes in an application.

  - **Boundary-value analysis**: When testing is done at the boundary level, or at the extreme limits (edges), it is referred to as boundary-value analysis. It is a very effective technique for finding defects. It's a condition where the limitations of the application's functions are identified and adding testing around those limitations gives positive or negative results. If it works around those conditions, that means precaution has been taken by developers, and if not, testers log it as a defect.

An example of boundary value would be to create a password field that accepts letters (A-Z) and numbers (0-9) with a minimum length of 6 and a maximum of 14 (that is, validating condition, if variable length <=6 and >=14, then throw error). In this case, testers can try to test this field by creating a password with the following:

- 5 characters
- 6 characters
- 7 characters
- 13 characters
- 14 characters
- 15 characters

It helps testers to identify whether it allows the user to create a password under or above the specified boundary range.

- **Equivalence partitioning**: Involves creating a small set of input values that can help generate a different set of output results. This helps with test coverage and reduces the work of the tester by verifying every single input value. This partition can consist of a set of the same values, different values, or a set of values with extreme conditions.

  For example, an insurance company has three types of subscription offers based on the users' age: the price is $100 per month if they're under 18, $250 if they're aged in the range 19-40, and $150 if they're older than 41. In this case, the input set of values can consist of the test data of users aged in the ranges 0-18, 18-20, 19-39, 35-40, 40-42, and above 41. It can also have some invalid input parameters, where age is 0, -1, a set letter (ABCD), decimal point values (33.45), three- or four-digit values (333 or 5,654), and so on.

- **White-box testing**: This is done at the code level for any software application. It involves verifying functions, loops, statements, its structure, the flow of data, expected output results based on a specified set of input values, as well as its internal design. A part of it is covered during the code-review process and unit testing to ensure the code coverage as per the specified requirements. Statement coverage, path coverage condition, and function coverage are all components of code coverage that help the reviewer to review every aspect of the code. With the help of white-box testing, we can identify the following things:
  - Unreachable parts of code, mostly created using `goto` statements
  - Variables (local or global) that have never been used or that store invalid values

- Memory leaks where memory allocation and deallocation for variables or pointers has been taken care of
- Whether a function returns values in the right type and expected format
- Whether all the required variables, pointers, classes, and objects are initialized as expected
- Whether the code is readable and follows the organization's coding conventions
- Whether the newly-added code functions as expected with the existing part of the code
- Whether the data flow is sequential and accurate
- Its efficiency and performance to optimize the code
- Resource utilization
- Whether all the configuration requirements have been met and include all the dependencies to run the component or the entire application

- **Integration testing:** Any piece of software is made of different modules or components and/or is used along with other software. In order to make sure that two or more individuals and independent units or components work together seamlessly, testers perform integration testing. This confirms that data across the different components of a system or two separate systems flows smoothly. An example of integration testing would be an online shopping website where selecting the item that you want to purchase and pay online using the internet-baking option, where you use your bank credentials to make a payment.

- **Performance testing:** The performance of an application is directly proportional to its business growth and value. Slow-performing applications are usually avoided by customers, which is why performance testing is important. It focuses on the factors that affect the performance of an application, product, or service, such as response time to perform any transaction or even load a page, throughput, and availability when a number of people are accessing it at the same time. On the other hand, if there are other jobs depending on one particular job that becomes slow or unresponsive, it delays all the dependent jobs and makes the situation even worse. Requirement specification documents should specify acceptable performance, limitations, and breaking situations. Performance testing can further be categorized into two components:

  - **Stress Testing**: Stress testing involves testing the **system under test** (**SUT**) under stress and reaching its breaking point. This helps testers to know under what circumstances the system will break and become unresponsive.

- **Load Testing**: Load testing involves testing the SUT under a specified heavy load, in order to make it withstand it and function as expected. An example would be a website that functions properly if there are 1,000 users accessing it simultaneous to upload photos up to 2 GB. It will break if there are more than 1,100 users accessing the website and uploading data that is more than 2 GB. Now, in this case, testers can create a set of concurrent users to access the website simultaneously and upload data greater than 2 GB, for example, using 1,110 users, 1,200 users and so on. The minute the system becomes unresponsive and stops working determines its breaking point. The point until which it can still respond and work becomes part of load testing.

- **Regression testing:** The main point of regression testing is to verify that newly-developed code or an updated version of code has no adverse effects on the existing and functioning part of the application. Sometimes, a newly designed part of an application or feature works perfectly but it breaks existing working functions. This is where regression testing comes into the picture.

  Regression testing is mostly done at the end of test cycles to ensure that the entire application—after making code changes multiple times due to bug fixes or an upgrade of any component of the code or database—still gives the desired results. Most of the time, testers use automated scripts to perform regression testing repetitively on the application. Tools such as HP-UFT, TestComplete, Eggplant, or Selenium with JUnit to NUnit are very useful for this type of testing.

- **Acceptance testing:** Confirms whether the software product or service is acceptable and functions as per the end user's expectations. Most organizations have **user acceptance testing** (**UAT**) as a separate phase of testing, which is generally conducted by a small group of end users or clients. The goal is to verify that the software product functions and meets customer needs, is safe to use, and has no ill effects on end users. It gives the development team an opportunity to incorporate any missing features or enhancement requests before releasing the product to a wider audience. At this stage, the client can still reject the product or its feature. When testing is carried out within the organization, mimicking a real-world environment setup, it's referred to as **Alpha testing**. When the acceptance test is carried out by end users in their own environments, it's referred to as **beta testing.** In this type of testing, the development team is not involved with the actual end users. This is a good test to share a beta version of a product with a relatively small group of actual end users so that they can verify the product, its functionality, and its features.

However, when releasing a beta version, it's important to list the hardware or software requirements. Along with that, a dedicated team of support executives should be made available to address customers' queries. Also, this version of the software could be made available for free for a limited time (generally, two weeks to a month) to encourage more people to participate in the actual test.

Preparing test data and managing test artifacts

In software testing, verifying test scenarios with valid or invalid parameters, and different sets of input values is crucial to make sure that it behaves as per the designed test. In order to validate end-to-end scenarios and happy path workflows, we need to create test data. However, sometimes, it's a requirement of the test to bring the system to the initial level from where testing can begin. All these things can be done as a part of the test data preparation phase.

Depending on system requirements, testers can create different sets of authorized and unauthorized users with different roles, such as admin, or customer support executive, all of whom have different sets of permissions to access the application. Creating a concurrent set of users to access the application is also part of test data preparation.

Testers may also have to use different types of files, such as `.doc`, `.docx`, `.txt`, `.pdf`, `.xls`, `.xlsx`, `.csv`, `.png`, or `.jpeg` to import the data in order to make sure that it works, or doesn't work as defined in the test case. In these files, they can add valid or invalid users, leave some fields blank, or add unacceptable values that will break the application or throw an error.

Testers also use these files as an input for their automated test scripts, which, in turn, do the job of test validation by inserting test data read from these input files.

Managing test artifacts

Managing test artifacts involves storing and managing the evidence that has been generated as a part of the test execution phase, or it can also be a set of deliverables generated after any phase of the SDLC.

These artifacts are very useful when managed properly:

- Artifacts generated during defect logging and retesting saves time for both developers and testers, preventing them from having to debug every part of the code, reproducing tests using specified test data, a build version and environment. Log error files, screenshots, database queries with the result set, input parameters, the URL of the application used during testing, the environment, the date tested on, the build number, and so on.
- Deliverables generated after the execution of each phase in the SDLC, such as project charters, BRDs, test plans, RTMs, and test execution reports, often serve as input to the subsequent phase and help teams to focus on the objective and track the progress of a project.
- Other types of artifacts, such as code review or inspection reports, project performance reports, and lessons learned reports, can be useful across the organization and can be used by other team members to make changes to their current strategy. These documents can be part of knowledge base of an organization.
- Training documents, templates (for project management plans, project charters, or requirement specifications) are also part of knowledge management and serve the training needs of new recruits to know more about the organization, its products, and standards followed by them.
- The end user's manual or product-specification documents are usually shared with end users, by the organization, to help them use software or services effectively.

The involvement of testers is not only limited to preparing test data but also preparing and building the knowledge base of an organization and making sure that all the information in the previously listed document is up to date and accurate.

Summary

In this chapter, we discussed software quality assurance in detail. Let's summarize the important points—a quality product refers to products that meet customer requirements. The ISO/IEC 25010:2011 quality model enumerates 13 characteristics that help us to assess the quality of products. Producing quality products requires a combination of complementary skills and roles as part of the product-development team. Scope, time, cost, and quality are intertwined, and hence a balance between them is essential when developing a product that caters to an organization's capabilities as well as customer satisfaction. A test-to-break attitude is necessary for a tester to be successful in their career. We looked at the thought process a tester needs to bring to the table to be proficient at the job. A quality management system addresses the processes to be followed to develop quality products. We discussed ISO 9001:2015 and CMMI v2.0 in detail. We looked at the five stages of the SDLC and learned how the STLC fits into the picture. We discussed the seven types of testing that a tester can utilize when planning tests based on customer and product needs. In the final section, we learned about how test data and artifacts are prepared, managed, retained, and shared for effective test management.

In the next chapter, we will look at project organization in Jira and explore the Zephyr, Test Management, and synapseRT plugins, which will be used to implement test management in Jira.

Section 2: Jira Environment - An Overview

We are going to learn how Jira can be used to organize and manage Agile Scrum and Kanban projects. We will also learn about Jira plugins, available from the Atlassian Marketplace that will help with test management.

This section will include the following chapters:

- Chapter 2, *Getting Started with Jira*
- Chapter 3, *Understanding Components of Testing with Jira*

Getting Started with Jira

2

The success of a project is the result of the approach adopted by the development team as it goes through each stage of the development process. To achieve success, the development team needs to have a good project manager at the helm who brings good project management skills and experience to be able to deliver a product that satisfies the end user's requirements. The project management process is organized into the following phases:

- Initiation
- Planning
- Execution
- Monitoring and controlling
- Closure

In this chapter, we will cover the following topics:

- What Jira is and how it can be used for project management
- How to set up Jira for the initiation and planning of a project
- An overview of the capabilities and features of three plugins—synapseRT, Zephyr, and Test Management

What is Jira?

Jira is a software tool, developed by a company named Atlassian in Australia, which provides an effective way to organize and manage your projects. It also provides capabilities to meet Agile project management needs.

Jira is like a container consisting of different types of Jira issues categorized under Jira projects. Using Jira, you can design, manage, and customize various types of tasks, workflows, and reports, and streamline the project management process. It helps to streamline the process of creating and managing project artifacts and provides a shared platform for project stakeholders to monitor project progress.

Jira boosts collaboration and productivity by doing the following:

- Reducing the effort spent tracking customer requirements manually
- Connecting team activities
- Providing different attributes that allow a team to divide requirements into contextual views, such as epics, components, issue types, tasks, sub tasks, and so on
- Generating different types of reports required by different user roles within team
- Interoperability with different plugins to help to take Jira to the next level and customize it as per their needs, such as the plugins for automation testing, manual test management, reporting, and so on

Organizing projects with Jira

Now that we have understood what Jira is, we can learn how to organize projects with it.

Jira can be used on the enterprise level to create different projects for various departments. While there is no rule of thumb for creating a project, deciding upon certain parameters can benefit organizations by segregating projects, which can aid in strategizing work effectively.

Agile project management using Jira

Organizations are moving away from traditional waterfall project management processes to iterative, fast, smooth, and systematic Agile project management processes. The Agile method for product development selects the most relevant requirements in each iteration or cycle and produces parts of the final product in each cycle.

Iterations are generally shorter and hence it is planned for a limited period. It provides the flexibility to reverse any new changes without affecting the larger product being developed. Thus, it helps to reduce the risk of failure and controls its impact. Comparing this to a traditional waterfall process, each development phase is complete but is interdependent on the previous phase.

This results in impacting the project timelines directly if any changes are introduced in the later phases. This interdependency, and longer periods of planning, result in a higher risk of failure, including cost and resources and overshooting the budget, and could possibly result in a product that doesn't meet the client's requirements. The following diagram shows a comparison of a waterfall process with an Agile process:

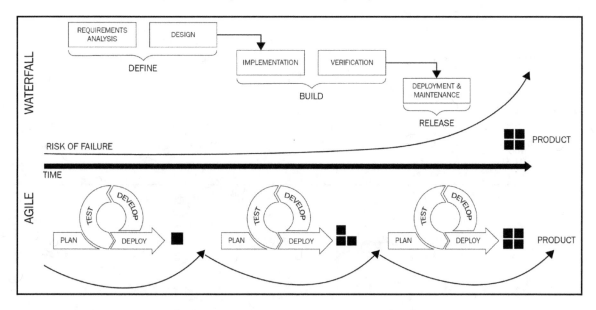

https://commons.wikimedia.org/wiki/File:Agile_Project_Management_by_Planbox.png and https://commons.wikimedia.org/wiki/File:Waterfall_model_(1).svg

The Agile method for product development provides greater flexibility with reduced dependencies. It helps teams to work in parallel on the roadmap outline, while being able to monitor and control each aspect of the deliverable based on the budget, skills, and resources of the team.

There are various types of Agile methodologies, such as:

- **Adaptive Software Development (ASD)**
- The crystal method
- **Dynamic System Development Method (DSDM)**
- The feature driver method
- Lean and Kanban software development
- **Extreme Programming (XP)**
- Scrum

Jira provides templates for the most widely used Agile methodologies—Scrum and Kanban. Let's explore the Scrum and Kanban methodologies and gain an understanding of common terminologies that help implement projects using Jira.

What is Scrum?

Scrum is a framework that helps to address customer needs and complex product requirements with the help of its adaptive, iterative, and systematic approach. It helps teams to deliver a product in different iterations, aligned as per the goals. As part of the product development effort, it gives an opportunity to define stakeholders' roles and organize their tasks, breaks down complex project scopes into smaller, understandable requirements, and provides a better way to integrate scope changes. The following diagram shows the phases and actors in the Agile Scrum methodology, which we will be looking at in detail next:

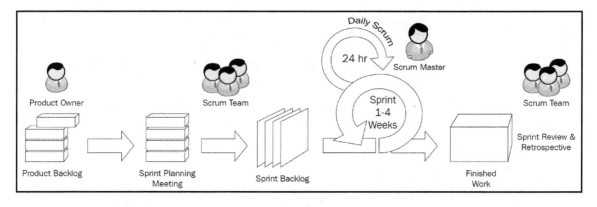

https://commons.wikimedia.org/wiki/File:Scrum_process.svg

Understanding Scrum in detail

Project requirements can be organized in Scrum using the Product Backlog and the Sprint Backlog:

- **Product Backlog**: This is a list of complex user requirements, wish lists, needs, and wants. The product owner is responsible for organizing and prioritizing this list, based on the customer's needs. It's a place where stakeholders can add requirements in the list anytime, but only the product owner is responsible for prioritizing and deleting the requirements. Hence, the Product Backlog is always in a growing phase.

- **Sprint Backlog**: Once the requirements are broken down into a smaller list of items, the team prepares and plans the list of tasks that need to be delivered in the only upcoming sprint. Such items are selected and added to the Sprint Backlog. Sprint planning meetings help the team to add story points to these selected tasks, based on their complexity, scope, and priority.

These artifacts help project stakeholders to track what is being asked, what is being implemented, and what has been delivered.

Scrum meetings

Scrum believes in collaboration and requires stakeholders to be a part of meetings to keep everyone aware and informed about items in scope, obstacles, dependencies, risks, resource availability, and so on, so that they can be planned for and addressed effectively.

There are five types of meetings that are crucial in Scrum:

- **Backlog refinement meeting**: Also referred to as Product Backlog grooming, which is conducted to give the product owner and the team some time to prepare, reorder, and organize backlog items before making commitments for the next sprint. Generally, a backlog grooming meeting is attended by the Scrum master, the product owner, and the development team.

- **Sprint planning**: This is an opportunity for all stakeholders to commit to the **Product Backlog Item (PBI)** and the relevant tasks that they will be completing as part of the upcoming sprint. These meetings help teams to identify user stories, to assign story points, and so on.

- **Sprint review:** It is important to validate whether user stories meet the scope and the acceptance criteria as specified and agreed by the team and whether they satisfy the customer's needs. Sprint review meetings are conducted to demonstrate the developed and tested product to the product owner.

- **Sprint retrospective**: Since Scrum is a continuous adaptive framework, it is necessary to understand what went right and what didn't. Sprint retrospective meetings provide an opportunity for all stakeholders to identify the scope of improvements and retain practices that worked well during the current sprint. This meeting is generally conducted at the end of the sprint.

- **Daily Scrum**: In order to respond to obstacles in a timely manner and track the progress of the project, it is important for all stakeholders to share the current status of any work items they are working on. Daily Scrum meetings are conducted to address such things and, as the name suggests, they happen daily (on average they are conducted for 15 minutes).

Readers can find more information about Scrum at this link: `https://www.scrumalliance.org/`.

What is Kanban?

Kanban is a continual delivery, lean-scheduling process focused on helping people work together more effectively as a team. The goal of both Kanban and Scrum is to deliver products just in time. However, Kanban uses the stages of the SDLC to track the progress of work items from requirement gathering to the delivery of the product or software. These different swim lanes are **BACKLOG**, **SELECTED FOR DEVELOPMENT**, **IN PROGRESS**, and **DONE**.

Unlike Scrum, Kanban doesn't follow an iterative approach and it has a long development period that is incremental in nature. Since there are no iterations, work items don't need to be started or ended at a specific time, rather, it depends on other factors, such as the priority of the work item, resource availability, the complexity of the requirements, and so on.

A Kanban board is used to track work items and their progress. It also helps teams to impose limits on the number of work items they want to add to the selected development stage. This enables smooth, consistent, and continuous delivery. By enabling limits, it reduces the overhead of managing or switching tasks between multiple items. A team can plan, estimate, design, and move each work item once it reaches the priority list of work items to deliver on it.

Project initiation and management

Now that we have understood the basics of Scrum and Kanban, let's discover how Jira helps us to create and manage our Agile projects using predefined project templates. We will be utilizing software development templates for Scrum and Kanban to plan our projects.

How to initiate projects in Jira

Jira provides flexibility for teams to organize project items based on their roles. We will be discussing these user roles and permissions in the next section. However, the admin role is the role with which we can create and set up a project as per our needs.

Setting up a Jira project is a very simple process. After you sign up, you will see the **Welcome!** page, where you can create projects from the templates provided, such as Scrum, Kanban, and so on.

Let's click on the **Create new project** button. It provides us with templates to create projects in **Software** or **Business**. In **Software**, we can see templates for **Basic software development**, **Scrum software development**, and **Kanban software development** projects. These are shown in the following screenshot:

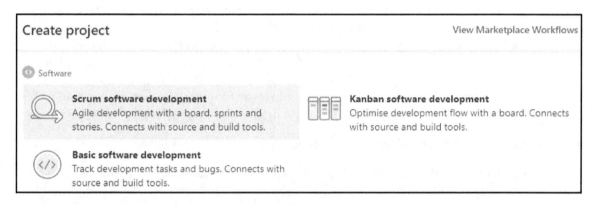

After project creation, there are a few more things that we need to take care of, such as configuring the project, the project dashboard, workflows, permissions, issue types, fields, components, and so on.

Apart from that, you may have to set up your project build repositories (from Fisheye or Bitbucket), as well as creating and configuring build plans. Also, Jira provides the flexibility to connect other development and team collaboration tools, such as Confluence, and HipChat.

Role-based permissions in Jira

Jira can be set up and configured for different user roles so that it satisfies the team's needs. An Agile project has various roles, such as Scrum master, development manager, product manager, project owner, team lead, developer, QA engineer, designer, technical writer, and so on. With the help of the admin user role, we can address the needs of each user group and customize Jira permissions accordingly.

There are three main types of permissions in Jira:

- **Global permission**: This is basically a user with admin permissions. It's a user who has access to all of the projects in Jira.
- **Project permission**: This is a restricted permission, limited to the selected project. Such users cannot access projects to which they do not have access. However, for any given project, they can create, edit, and manage project issues and assign them back and forth to other team members.
- **Issue security permission**: This is restricted access on the issue type level to provide access to a limited audience only. Jira is a ticket-based system and you can create different types of tickets or issues and restrict their access using Issue Security Permission. For example, if the issue type is Epic, then you can add only managers in the list to be able to view Epic issue type tickets.

However, there are admins on each level of these permissions, as follows:

- **Jira administrator**: This is an role where the user can customize, manage, and configure Jira
- **Project administrator**: The project administrator can take control of sprint related tasks, such as creating, starting, moving, editing, end, deleting, completing, and renaming sprints
- **Board administrator**: The board administrator can control the dashboard by creating a board, modifying workflows, adding/removing a status, and so on

 Make sure you are aware of your project needs. Make sure you know well in advance what issue types your team might need, and the types of default or customized workflows, fields, or components that the team wants to use.

In the next section, we will be creating and managing projects with the Jira admin user role.

Scrum using Jira

Let's start by creating a Scrum project in Jira:

1. Once you select the **Scrum software development** option, it takes you to the following page. The listed **Issue Types** will be available as default **Issue Types** for your project with the specified default **workflow**. Remember, you can always add new or modify existing issue types and workflows. This is shown in the following screenshot:

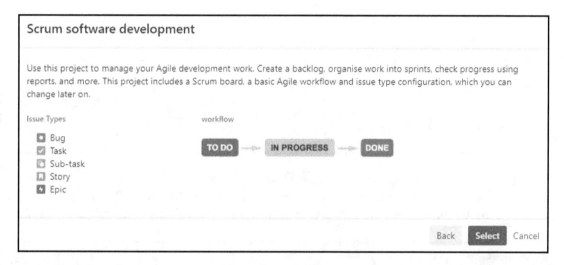

2. Provide a **Name** for your project with a **Key** and assign the **Project Lead**, as shown in the following screenshot:

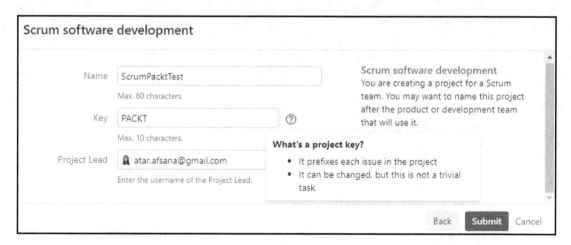

3. On clicking **Submit**, the project will be created, and you will see the project **Backlog** page, as shown in the following screenshot:

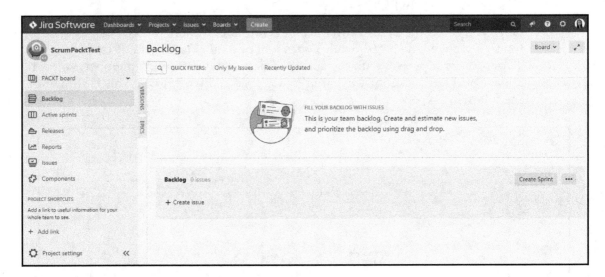

4. Now, you are ready to add project backlog items by creating issues and plans, and organize them by creating sprints and starting iterations. The following screenshot shows a sample active Scrum project for **Sample Sprint 2**:

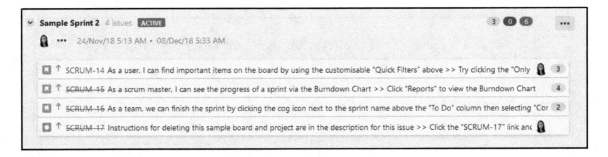

Kanban using Jira

Now let's create a Kanban project in Jira:

1. Once you select the **Kanban software development** option, it takes you to the following page:

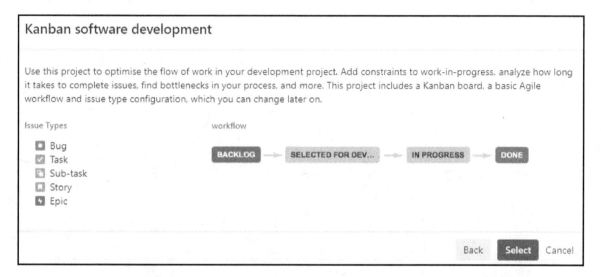

The listed **Issue Types** will be available as default **Issue Types** for your Kanban project with the specified default **workflow**. As mentioned earlier, you can always add new or modify existing issue types and workflows.

2. Create a Kanban project by specifying the **Name and Key**, and assigning the **Project Lead.**
3. On clicking **Submit**, the Kanban project will be created, and you will see the **Kanban board.**

4. Now you are ready to add project items by creating issues, planning and organizing it in the swim lanes. The following screenshot shows a **Kanban board** with requirements going through different swim lanes, such as **BACKLOG**, **SELECTED FOR DEVELOPMENT**, **IN PROGRESS**, and **DONE**:

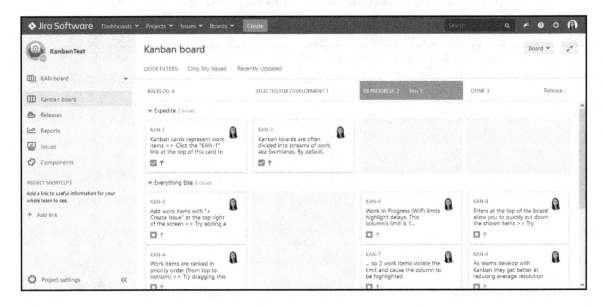

Now we are ready with our project, let's explore the plugins supported by Jira to understand the test management aspect of it.

Exploring test management plugins for Jira

The test management process helps to organize, track, and manage testing-related project needs. There are various phases that software development goes through, and testing has its own segregated set of phases. Each of these phases has a set of activities through which we can track the progress of a project, such as creating test plans and test cases, organizing them into test suites, creating test cycles, managing execution, creating and retesting defects, and so on. STLC and its integration with the SDLC was covered in Chapter 1, *An Overview of Software Quality Assurance*.

In the upcoming sections, we will learn in detail about the different test management phases, such as manage, plan, design, and execute, as well as how to monitor and control test cases with the help of Jira plugins.

In the following section, we will get an overview of each of the plugins supported by Jira. So, let's get started.

synapseRT

synapseRT is a Jira app which supports end-to-end testing and requirement management with Jira. It's a plugin that integrates smoothly with the Jira environment to extend its capabilities by enabling testers, test managers, and project managers to plan, execute, and track the progress of a project throughout the SDLC. It organizes the entire test process into four sections:

- **Test case**: This section is where testers can design and maintain test cases. It also provides the flexibility to reuse them whenever needed.
- **Test execution**: This is the phase where testers can design and plan the test strategy required for the current release, as per the scope of the testing.
- **Test automation**: synapseRT integrates smoothly with other third-party automation or continuous integration tools, with the help of which test professionals can execute automated scripts and get the status of execution.
- **Requirements**: In terms of requirement management, it is essential for the team to track the progress of the project so that the allocation and distribution of resources is easy. Also, this helps in the identification and mitigation of risks in the early stages of testing. Traceability reports generated by synapseRT are very useful for this.

In the upcoming chapters, we will be going through every section of synapseRT in detail and will explore its use, as well as best practices. In this section, let's install synapseRT in Jira and learn about the basic configuration settings needed to get started.

Jira can be customized as per the user's needs, and so can synapseRT. It provides the flexibility to design customized workflows and to add issue types or even fields. You can install synapseRT from the Atlassian Marketplace.

Simply log in to Jira and search for synapseRT in the **Add-ons** section. Its free-trial version is available to explore before purchasing. The current version of synapseRT (v9.3.1) has been used for this book. After enabling the plugin, the Jira project explorer adds the **Requirements**, **Test Suites**, and **Test Plans** options. In the following screenshots, you will see the before and after installation screens:

In order to view the synapseRT fields for the issue type (which is the requirement in your case), such as **Epic**, **Story**, **Task** and so on you need to configure it as follows:

 Defect issue type is a new issue type that we will learn how to add in the upcoming chapters.

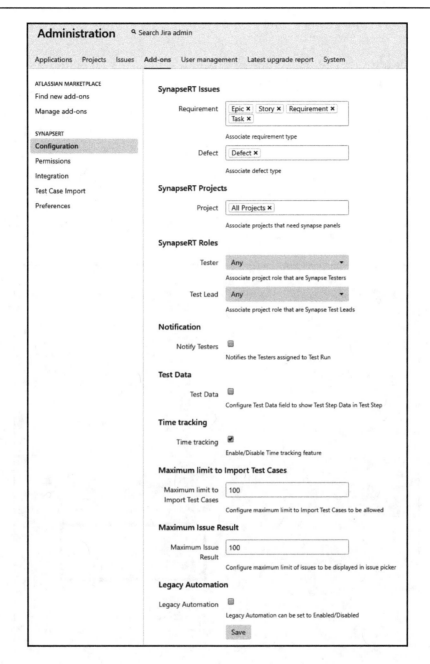

Here is a link for getting to know the supported version of synapseRT that works with Jira: https://doc.go2group.com/synapsert/latest/en/synapsert-ver-9-x/supported-jira-versions.

Zephyr

Zephyr for Jira is another test management tool supported by Jira. Just like synapseRT, it can be used to design and organize test cases. It helps testers to plan test execution and to manage custom fields on a global level, or on a project level. With the help of an Agile test board, teams can manage and report on the progress of work. It also supports advanced search options using the **Zephyr Query Language (ZQL)**. It can be integrated easily with other automation tools, as well as continuous integration tools with ZAPI.

Zephyr is available to download from the Atlassian Marketplace. The current version of Zephyr (v4.0.2) has been used for this book.

In the following screenshots, you will see the before and after installation scenarios as it adds extra components to the left-hand side menu:

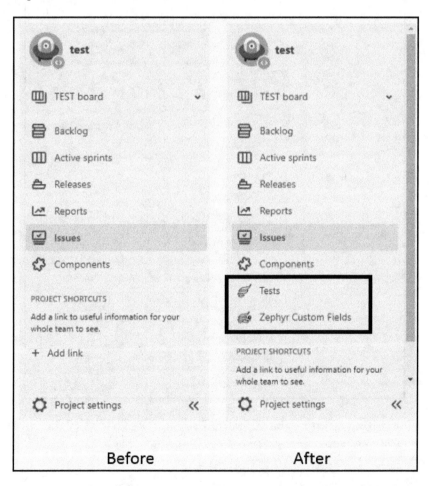

In order to view Zephyr fields for the issue type (whichever is the requirement in your case, for example, **Epic**, **Story**, **Task**, and so on), you need to configure it as follows:

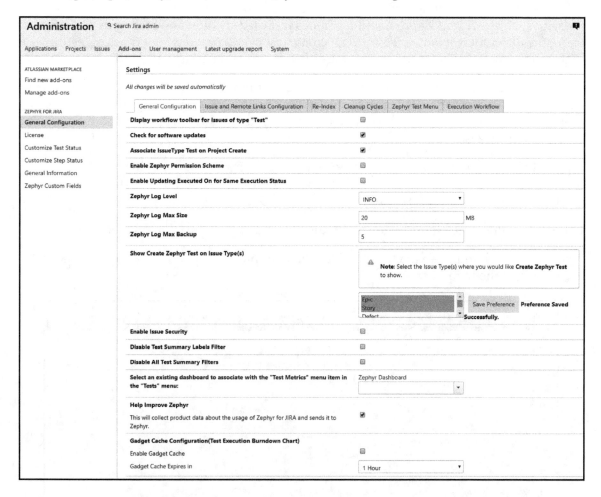

Here is a link for getting to know the supported version of Zephyr that works with Jira: https://marketplace.atlassian.com/apps/1014681/zephyr-for-jira-test-management/version-history.

Test Management

The Test Management plugin is another tool supported by Jira. It has similar components to those of synapseRT and Zephyr, and facilitates test case creation and managing test cases using the different test suites. Testers can create test cycles based on the types of testing required for the selected requirement, for different browsers' tests, and so on.

It is possible to track the requirements for defects with the help of a traceability matrix. It extends the support for automation tools and DevOps tools using the REST API. The Test Management tool is available to use in localized languages such as English, German, Spanish, Portuguese, and Italian.

The Test Management tool is available to download from the Atlassian Marketplace (`https://marketplace.atlassian.com/`). The current version of the Test Management tool (v5.1.1) has been used for this book.

In the following screenshots, you will see the before and after installation scenarios.

Before installing and enabling the Test Management plugin, the Jira project doesn't have a **Tests** tab in the menu bar:

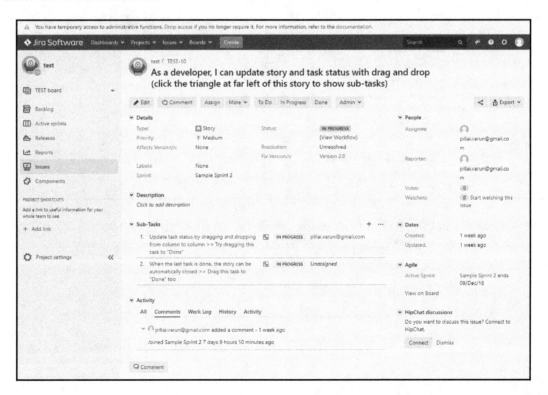

As you can see, it added a tab called **Tests** and **Test Management for Jira** on the **Administration** dropdown:

In order to view the Test Management tool for the issue type (which is the requirement in your case), such as Epic, Story, Task, and so on) you will need to enable it. On enabling the plugin for your project, you will be able to create tests for the project from the **Tests** tab as follows:

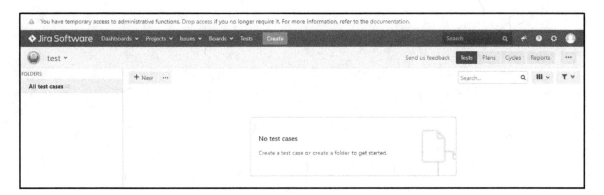

Summary

In this chapter, we learned about Jira and plugins supported by Jira to meet your Agile projects' needs. Jira is a project management tool that provides various templates to create and manage your project artifacts. Scrum and Kanban are the two most widely used Agile project management methodologies. Jira supports both methodologies and provides tools to meet your test management needs. Using simple steps, you can create and manage your projects in Jira and restrict access to information using the different sets of permissions and roles. We explored the workflow to create projects in Scrum and Kanban. In the final section, we explored the installation and configuration of three test management plugins—synapseRT, Zephyr, and Test Management.

In the next chapter, we will cover in detail how each phase of test management can be performed using the Test Management plugins in Jira. We will also compare the features provided by each plugin.

3
Understanding Components of Testing with Jira

Requirements, test suites, a test plan, traceability, and reports are the main components of testing provided as part of the Jira test management solution. Test suites, also known as test repositories, are used to organize test cases. Test planning is an important factor before we move on to the test execution phase. Traceability and reports help us to track the coverage and progress of the testing efforts in a project-release cycle.

In this chapter, we will cover the approach of Test Management using its plugins in Jira. First, we'll understand the requirements and some basics of a test plan, along with issue types, including the default workflow that every issue type goes through in Jira. We'll learn to create customized workflows and add them to the project using workflow schemes. Then we'll create our own issue type and apply this newly-created workflow to that issue type. We'll also take a look at issue types in detail and compare the test suite features provided by all three plugins. We'll start by understanding some basics of the test plan and where it resides in Jira plugins.

In this chapter, we'll look at the following topics in detail:

- What are requirements?
- Issue types
- What is test suite and what are its advantages?
- What is test plan?
- What is a traceability matrix and what are its benefits?
- Reports and their types

Requirements

Requirements are basically parts of the solution that will help you solve the end user's problems. They can also be desirable items that will attract the end user to use the product or service. Further, requirements may also contain functions that might be widely used in the existing products available in the market, which makes it critical to be available for a new product to enter the market.

What are requirements?

Requirements can be a functional/non-functional and implicit/explicit list of features. Either way, they basically get classified as either core needs or good-to-haves for a product or service that will satisfy the customer. The specification varies on the target audience and the type of product being developed by the organization.

In the software industry, once the project is formally initiated and is allocated to a software development team, the first task for the project stakeholder is to gather the requirements. Gathering requirements helps the team to understand the scope of the project, timeline, budget, supported technology, its limitations, number of resources required, features requested, the customer's wish list, and so on.

After the requirements are gathered and documented, the project coordinator (who acts as a liaison between the end user and the software development team) gets it approved from the end user. On receiving the go-ahead for the development phase, the requirements are analyzed and broken down into smaller work packets that become tasks for the team. Jira provides an effective way to help the team to organize and manage these tasks.

Jira was built as a ticket-based system, where each task is represented as a ticket. Thus, requirements that are tasks for the team become a ticket in Jira. Jira also allows for the classification of tasks utilizing issue types (which basically helps in categorizing requirements to segregate work). Every Jira project has supported issue types by default. Now, if you're wondering whether your project supports an issue type, this can be confirmed on the first screen when creating a new project:

The default **Issue Types** that are seen in the preceding screenshot are **Bug**, **Task**, **Sub-task**, **Story**, and **Epic**. Jira also provides flexibility to customize the supported issue types for a project by adding, editing, and/or deleting issue types, as well as workflows. If the project or organization requires further segregation and classification of items in the project beyond what's available by default, then team members can create their own issue types as well, which we'll see in the following section.

In Chapter 9, *Requirement Management,* we'll learn how to configure Jira issue types as requirements for testing. We'll also use these issue types to link with relevant test cases using Jira plugins.

Issue types

Creating and using a new issue type involves the following six steps:

1. Log in as Admin, navigate to **Administration** | **Issues** | **Add issue type**, and follow the steps from the official documentation (*Defining issue type field values*: https://confluence.atlassian.com/adminjiraserver/defining-issue-type-field-values-938847087.html) to add a new issue type. We have created a new issue type named ProdIssue:

2. Let's create a new workflow for `ProdIssue`. To create a new workflow, log in as `Admin`, navigate to **Administration** | **Workflows** | **Add Workflow**, and follow the steps from the official documentation (*Working with workflows*: `https:/ /confluence.atlassian.com/adminjiraserver072/working-with-workflows- 828787890.html`):

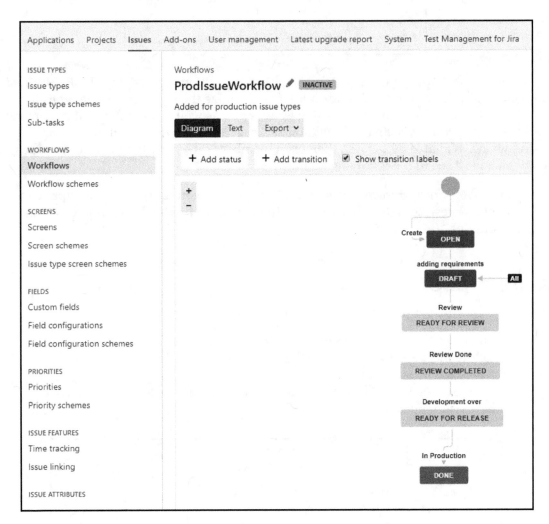

3. Let's navigate to **Administration** | **Workflow schemes** | **Add Workflow scheme** and create a new workflow scheme:

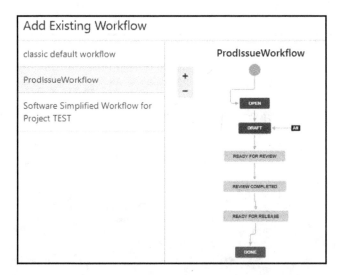

4. Select the desired workflow scheme and click **Add Workflow** | **Add Existing** to add our `ProdIssueWorkflow` workflow to the workflow scheme.

5. Select the `ProdIssue` issue type from the list to which of issue types that you want to assign to this workflow:

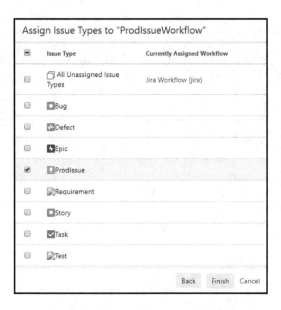

6. Let's add the new `ProdIssue` issue type to this project by navigating to **Administration** | **Issues** | **Issue type schemes** and selecting the scheme for your current project:

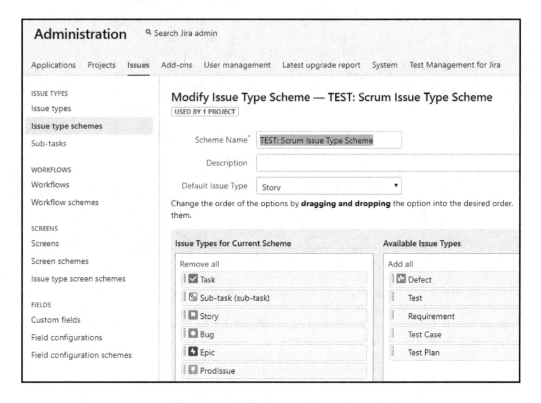

Don't forget to click on **Publish Workflows** to reflect the changes in your project. Now, if you check your project, you'll see the new `ProdIssue` issue type:

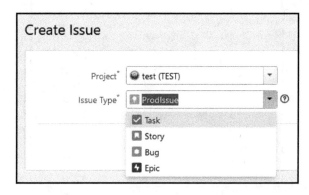

Test suites

When a software development company gets a big project, it must split the project into smaller components so that it can apply the *divide-and-conquer* strategy. The final product is then created by integrating these smaller components. The general procedure for dividing the bigger project is by grouping requirements for a common feature together to form smaller projects. Each of these smaller projects then get assigned to a development team. Thus, each team works on delivering part of the larger final product:

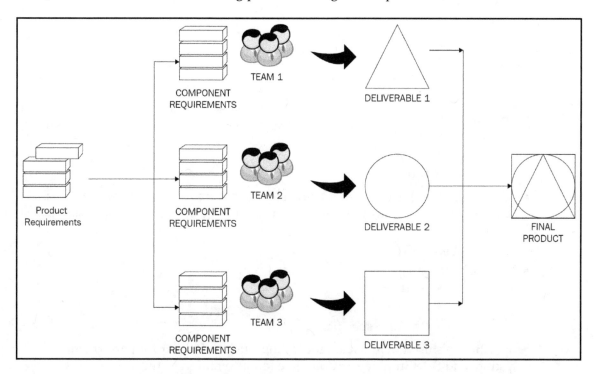

Testing efforts for each of these projects starts with the testers creating test scenarios and test cases. The number and complexity of the test cases vary with the size, duration, complexity, testing tools utilized, and the testing strategy. The biggest challenge, however, is to segregate these test cases so that they're easily accessible and can be referred to or reused across projects or organization-wide. This is where the concept of test suites comes in handy.

What is a test suite?

A **test suite** is simply a bucket that holds a collection of test cases with similar behaviors or goals. Each test suite has common characteristics defined by underlying test cases and varies in numbers.

Various characteristics contribute towards recognizing and distinguishing the patterns of test suites, namely, the following:

- Requirements.
- Priority:
  - High
  - Low
  - Critical
- Components.
- Test environment:
  - Development
  - Test
  - Production
- Test input parameters or type. These include different sets or types of values, such as .csv files, images, variables, objects, or even returned values from functions.
- Expected behavior.
- Type of testing:
  - Regression
  - Smoke
  - Browser-specific
- Specific tools used by the team for testing, such as Fiddler for performance testing, and Selenium or TestComplete for automation testing.
- Prerequisites is a state from which you can start testing; for example, an account must be created in order to log in.

Test suites are usually created by grouping test cases related to a requirement. Since the bigger project has already been split based on common requirements, test suites should also be created in line with those same modules. This will help us to identify test cases relevant to the requirements.

So, if in future, certain requirements receive changes, the corresponding test cases can easily be identified and targeted for maintenance and quality. So, the same thought process applies when organizing test cases based on the other categories listed previously as well.

Let's consider an example of an online banking website. It has various sections, and each section has its own modules, as follows:

- Banking:
  - Checking
  - Saving
- Insurance:
  - Car
  - Home
  - Personal
- Loan:
  - Car
  - Home
  - Personal mortgage
- Investment:
  - Brokerage account
  - Retirement plans for 403K and 401K
  - Mutual funds
- Card:
  - Credit cards
  - Debit cards

In such cases, categorizing them based on the preceding factors is an effective way to not only build a well-managed test suite, but also to organize and reuse it. Hence, it's a good strategy to create a main category and some subcategories under it, to differentiate each testing component separately. So, let's look at an example of test suites in Jira for each of the plugins in the following sections.

The test suite in synapseRT

In synapseRT, the **Test Suites** tab is displayed on the left panel of the project page. From this section, we can create and manage test cases in the form of main and subtest suites. The following screenshot shows the main test suite, `Mobile banking App Tests`, which has a total of four test cases that have been organized into two subtest suites—`IOS device test` and `Android device test`. We also have the option to clone test cases from one test suite to another, delete, or even export test cases:

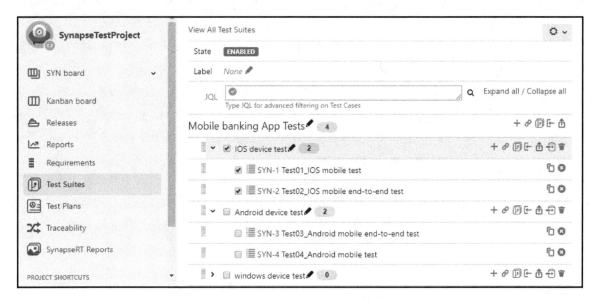

The test suite in Zephyr

Zephyr provides a way to manage your test execution with the help of test cycles. However, it doesn't provide a feature to organize test cases by test suites. The **Test Summary** screen provides a detailed view of the number of test cases, organized by version, component, or label, and their execution status:

The test suite in Test Management

Click on the **Tests** tab and create a new folder in the **FOLDERS** section. These folders will be your test suites. You can add new test cases by clicking the +**New** button on the screen. We have created a few test suites and test cases for our banking example, shown as follows:

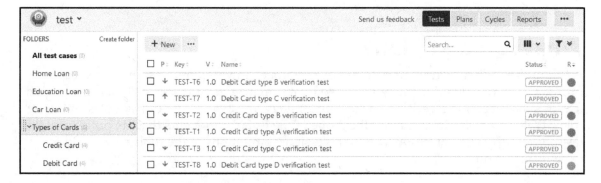

For the preceding banking example, testers can also create test suites at a high level based on mobile testing, web application testing, credit card testing, personal banking testing, account types testing, load types testing, and so on.

Advantages of test suites

It's beneficial for test professionals to have organized test suites for the following reasons:

- It helps to separate the types of tasks that need to be performed for the verification of requirements
- The effort estimation in terms of time and resource requirements is made easy
- It acts as a knowledge-base repository
- It makes it easy to identify test cases to mitigate risk
- The identification and retesting of previously released components is made easy

Test suites often grow as a project progresses. Well-organized test suites are essential for effective test management.

Test plans

Planning is important if you want to be successful in delivering a project. We plan for each activity at each phase of the development process. Testing is no different. To ensure the quality of the product and perform verification, a test plan is crucial.

What is a test plan?

A test plan is a document that outlines your approach to verify and test the software product. It's a detailed document prepared by test managers or test leads that highlights the features that need to be verified, the testing strategy, the availability of resources, and their roles. It also contains details about the scope of the test, components that are not part of the test phase, supported browser types and versions, limitations of the tools being used for testing, and so on.

Every phase in the SDLC generates a set of deliverables. For example, the requirement gathering phase generates the BRD, the design phase generates high-level and low-level system and component design plans, and the test planning phase generates a test plan. A test professional uses the test plan, along with the BRD, in the test-case creation phase to create use cases and test scenarios. Organizations that have quality certifications, such as CMMI, usually have standard templates for such documents. Organizations also recommend having test plans on a high level and testing level for cases where testing is conducted across multiple departments.

Consider the upgrade of an organization-wide database, which might affect several departments, such as HR, finance, technology, sales, support, and the front desk. In this scenario, it's beneficial for the test professionals to prepare one master test plan and several other test plans for each individual department that's part of the same upgrade project. Let's see where this test plan section resides in each of the Jira plugins.

The test plan in synapseRT

The **Test Plan** is another issue type in synapseRT. On clicking on the **Create** button, we get an option to choose the issue type as **Test Plan**. Once we enter all the details and create our test plan, we can add test cases and test cycles, as shown in the following screenshot. synapseRT provides an effective way of managing test cycles using the test plan. You can always add or remove test cases from the selected cycles before starting the execution.

However, once the cycle starts, a user can only add new test cases to the test cycles:

The test plan in Zephyr

Zephyr uses the **Cycle Summary** to plan the test cycle. Once cycles are planned, the test team can add and remove test cases from the cycles as needed. Test cases are validated for the content and, details, and assigned to the teams for peer review. After the peer review, it can be marked as **Ready to Test** and assigned to the team members who will be responsible for the execution of the test cases. Once the cycles with the updated test cases are ready, it can be moved under the targeted release test cycle and the team can start the execution phase. The following screenshot shows how test cycles are planned:

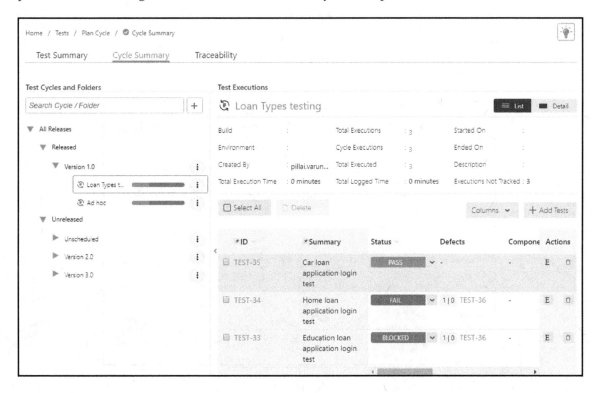

The test plan in Test Management

Test Management provides a tab named **Plans** to create and manage test plans:

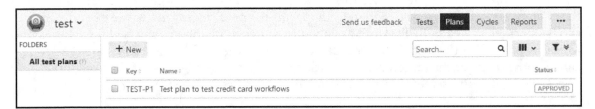

Once you create a test plan, you can add test cycles, which contain test cases, as shown in the following screenshot. This can then be viewed from the **Traceability** section of the test plan:

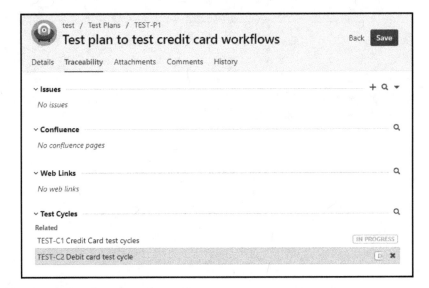

Traceability

Requirements are usually documented in the BRD, **software requirement and specifications (SRS)** document, or in the **Requirements** section of the project management tools, such as Jira, being used by the team. Test scenarios and test cases are created in order to verify the stated requirements. It's important to ensure and track that all the requirements have corresponding test cases and are covered in the testing and verification phases. This is what the traceability matrix helps us manage.

What is a traceability matrix?

The traceability matrix, also known as the **Requirement Traceability Matrix (RTM)**, is a document that helps test professionals to establish a correlation between what they are being asked to test and what is being covered in the testing phase. It establishes a many-to-many relationship between the requirements and the test scenarios or test cases identified, which will be used to verify the linked requirements. The traceability matrix helps us to identify any leaks in quality and ensures complete test coverage so that no part of the requirements missed from the test.

Once the execution phase begins, the test professionals start the application-validation process by following the detailed steps mentioned in the test cases. The main goal is to identify whether a module satisfies conditions and meets the expected results. If it does, the test is passed, and if it doesn't, we call it a **defect**. The number of defects may vary from one execution cycle to another.

It's important for project stakeholders to be aware of the status of the test execution, so that they understand which requirements are yet to be verified and can address the obstacles in time. When raising a defect in the system, if it's linked to the relevant test case, it's easy to trace the defect back to the test cases, which can then be traced back to the given requirement. Often, in the case of the traceability matrix, it's important to add the test execution status, as well as linked defects' details. There are various formats of the RTM available that can help establish this relationship between the requirement being tested and the test cases and related defects.

Types of traceability matrices

The most popular types of the RTM are shown in the following examples:

- **Forward traceability matrix:** This is where requirements are linked to the test cases:

Business requirement ID#	Use case ID#	Priority	Test case ID#
BR_1	UC_1	High	TC#001
	UC_2	High	TC#002 TC#005
BR_2	UC_3	Medium	TC#003 TC#004

- **Backward traceability matrix**: This is where test cases are mapped to the requirements:

Test case ID#	Use case ID#	Priority	Business requirement ID#
TC#001	UC_1	High	BR_1
TC#002	UC_2	High	BR_1
TC#003	UC_3	Medium	BR_2
TC#004	UC_3	Medium	BR_2
TC#005	UC_1	High	BR_1

- **Bi-directional traceability matrix**: This is where both forward and backward traceability is possible, which makes it easy to trace requirements to test cases and vice versa:

	Business requirement ID#	BR_1		BR_2
	Use case ID#	UC#1	UC#2	UC#3
Priority	Test case ID#			
High	TC#001	×		
High	TC#002		×	
Medium	TC#003			×
Medium	TC#004			×
High	TC#005	×		

Benefits of the traceability matrix

The following are the benefits of the traceability matrix:

- It makes it easy to track the status of test execution
- It helps to ensure whether the test scenarios provide complete test coverage before the test execution begins
- It identifies which requirements need more testing efforts in terms of resource allocation, time, debugging, or defect resolution time
- It addresses and resolves issues ahead of time to reduce their impact on the project
- It monitors the project's progress and estimates completion time well in advance by reducing the risk of failure

In `Chapter 8`, *Defect Management Phase,* we'll see how to link defects to the test cases, and in `Chapter 9`, *Requirement Management,* we'll learn how to link requirements to the test cases. For now, let's see how each Jira plugin generates the traceability report.

Traceability in synapseRT

The traceability matrix in synapseRT can be generated from the **Traceability** tab on the left panel of the page. We have to enter the details, such as requirements (Epic, Task, Story, or Requirement) or project, and the relevant test plan (if any exists), for which we want to generate a traceability matrix. The following screenshot shows a forward traceability matrix generated in synapseRT. It shows the details, such as the requirements, their relevant test cases, their current execution status, and any linked defects. We also have an option to view traceability as a **Matrix** or **Tree**:

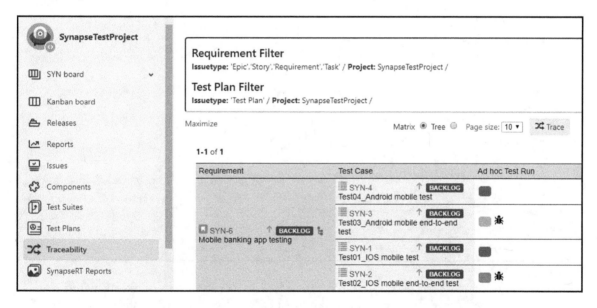

Traceability in Zephyr

Zephyr provides both, forward and backward traceability reports. Let's understand how to create them in detail:

1. To create a forward traceability matrix, specify the current version and select the requirement issue type from the list, such as **Epic**, **Story**, or **Tasks**, and click on the search icon. Based on the input parameters, Zephyr lists the relevant issue types on the page. Select the checkbox for the issue and the **Requirements to Defects** for which you want to generate the traceability matrix:

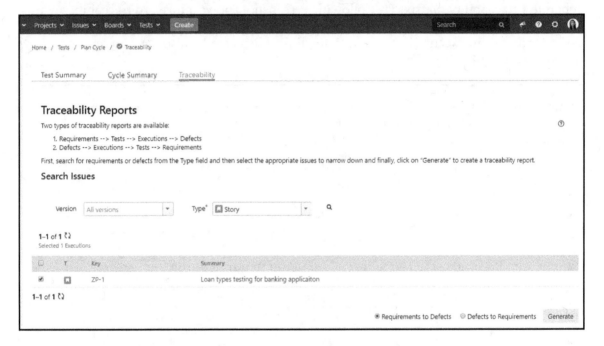

2. The forward traceability matrix generated in Zephyr shows a relationship between requirements, their linked test cases, their execution status, and linked defects. We have a requirement, ZP-1, and there are three test cases added to this requirement. The **Executions** column shows further details about the execution status of each test case, for example, as a test case, ZP-9 has two executions and both times it failed. It also has a linked defect, ZP-11, added in the **Defects** column:

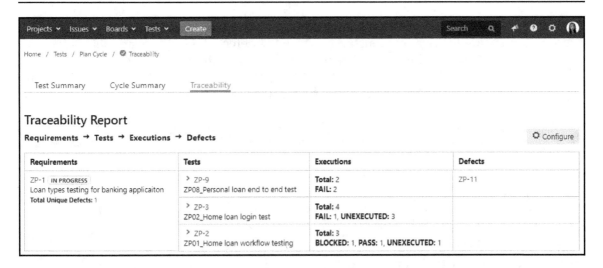

3. Use the preceding steps to generate the backward traceability matrix. In this case, we will select the issue type as **Bug**, which we want to generate a traceability matrix for Zephyr shows all the relevant bug issues on the screen—select the one for which you want to generate the traceability, select the type as **Defect to Requirements**, and click on the **Generate** button:

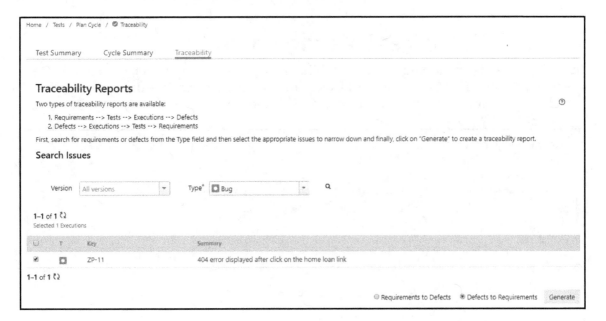

4. As shown in the following screenshot, we have a backward traceability matrix that establishes a relationship between the defect of a test case and its relevant requirements. This matrix has the **Defects**, **Executions**, **Tests**, and **Requirements** columns with the linked Jira issues. In both the cases, we have an option to export the traceability in HTML or Excel formats:

Traceability in Test Management

In the Test Management plugin, the traceability report details the **Coverage**, which shows the requirements; **Test Cases** and **Test Executions** results, showing the details about the test case; and **Issues**, which details the defects found during test execution:

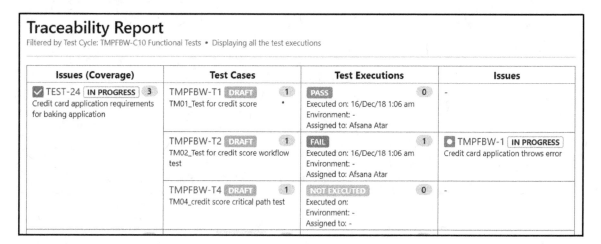

Reports

Reports are a formalized way of effectively and regularly communicating the status of the project's progress. They play a key role in the project management process. Details provided in the reports are helpful in identifying and mitigating the risks that might lead to the failure of the project.

Reports act as a project health-checker and help managers to track any deviation from the agreed scope, time, cost, budget, and stated resource requirements necessary to meet the quality. These reports also act as reference documents as a part of the knowledge base that can be maintained and shared within an organization.

Types of reports

Reporting needs vary based on the targeted audience. Jira reports are helpful to determine the statistics of the project and can be customized based on the people, projects, versions, or issue types that we will be exploring here. In `Chapter 10`, *Test Execution Status Reporting*, we'll explore the different types of reports supported by Jira plugins. For now, let's look at the types of reports supported by Jira:

- **Agile**: Agile reports are useful to track the progress of the project by generating various types of reports. It gives more insights into the project and helps the project team to address the issues in time. It helps to compare and contract the projected timelines for the project.
    - **Burndown Chart**: This graph helps to differentiate between the total work completed and the work needed to be completed for the selected project.
    - **Sprint Report**: If the project has one or more sprints, by using the sprint reports, the team can estimate the efforts for the selected sprint. It helps to reorganize efforts based on the timeline and resource capacity.
    - **Velocity Chart**: This helps to foresee the team's velocity and planned future sprints based on the team's capacity achieved in the previous sprints.
    - **Cumulative Flow Diagram**: This helps to track the progress of issues over the duration of the project. It can be helpful to identify obstacles if any are causing delays in the project's progress.
    - **Version Report**: If a project is being released in different versions, version reports are helpful to track the progress of the selected version of the product.

- **Epic Report**: This report helps to track the progress of the epic over time.
- **Control Chart**: This helps to identify the average time spent by the particular issue in a particular state.
- **Epic Burndown**: This tracks the progress of all the sprints planned for the selected project.
- **Release Burndown**: It can be helpful to know the progress of the project for the targeted release.

The aforementioned reports can be generated from **Reports | Agile** section as shown in the following screenshot. Along with the report name it also has a short description and sample graph image to provide more details about the report to the users:

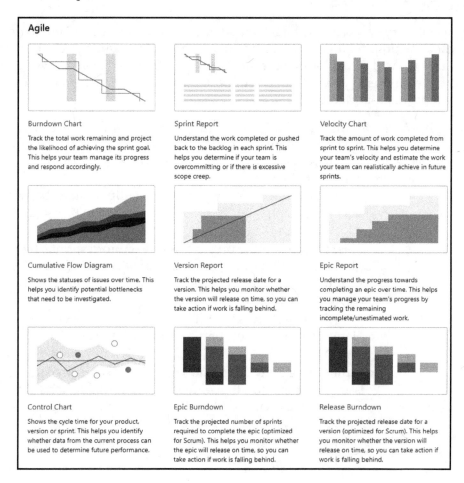

Agile

Burndown Chart

Track the total work remaining and project the likelihood of achieving the sprint goal. This helps your team manage its progress and respond accordingly.

Sprint Report

Understand the work completed or pushed back to the backlog in each sprint. This helps you determine if your team is overcommitting or if there is excessive scope creep.

Velocity Chart

Track the amount of work completed from sprint to sprint. This helps you determine your team's velocity and estimate the work your team can realistically achieve in future sprints.

Cumulative Flow Diagram

Shows the statuses of issues over time. This helps you identify potential bottlenecks that need to be investigated.

Version Report

Track the projected release date for a version. This helps you monitor whether the version will release on time, so you can take action if work is falling behind.

Epic Report

Understand the progress towards completing an epic over time. This helps you manage your team's progress by tracking the remaining incomplete/unestimated work.

Control Chart

Shows the cycle time for your product, version or sprint. This helps you identify whether data from the current process can be used to determine future performance.

Epic Burndown

Track the projected number of sprints required to complete the epic (optimized for Scrum). This helps you monitor whether the epic will release on time, so you can take action if work is falling behind.

Release Burndown

Track the projected release date for a version (optimized for Scrum). This helps you monitor whether the version will release on time, so you can take action if work is falling behind.

- **Issue analysis**: Issue analysis reports are helpful to track the issue progress from creation to the closure phase. It helps to know the details such as logging time, resolution details and the duration since it was created and so on.

    - **Average Age Report**: This tracks the status of the pending items that have been in the same states.
    - **Created vs. Resolved Issues Report**: This report helps to compare issues with created and completed statuses.
    - **Pie Chart Report**: With the help of a pie chart report, we can view the status of the issue grouped by the assignee, or other filter conditions, for a selected sprint or project.
    - **Recently Created Issues Report**: This report helps to compare the issues when the selected project is at the created and completed statuses.
    - **Resolution Time Report**: This helps to track the time that a team member has spent to resolve/complete the selected issue.
    - **Single Level Group By Report**: As the name suggests. this report is helpful to add a condition and view the status of the report based on the selected condition. It helps to further narrow down the search results.
    - **Time Since Issues Report**: This shows a bar chart with the number of issues based on the added conditions, such as created date or resolved date.

As shown in the following screenshot, **Issue analysis** section of the report, lists the reports as discussed previously. Along with the report name it also provides a short description and sample graph image to get a clear understanding of the report type:

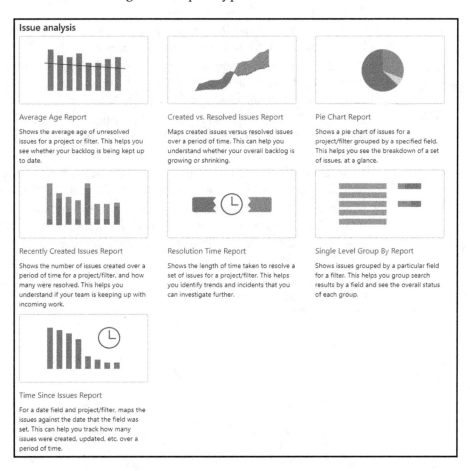

- **Forecast-management report**: Forecast Management reports are useful to track the progress of the project and check the timelines. It helps to track the time, the workload on the project team and so on.
    - **Time Tracking Report**: This report helps to differentiate between the planned and actual estimates for issues of the selected project
    - **User Workload Report**: Helps to track the workload based on the resources
    - **Version Workload Report**: Generates a version-specific report with assigned users and related issues

As shown in the following screenshot, **Forecast & management** reports can be generated from **Reports | Forecast & management** section. Along with the report name, it adds a short description of about the report and a sample graph to understand the report types and style more clearly:

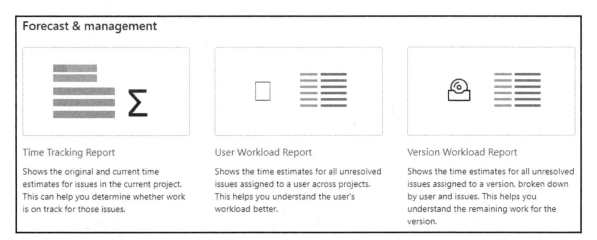

Forecast & management

Time Tracking Report

Shows the original and current time estimates for issues in the current project. This can help you determine whether work is on track for those issues.

User Workload Report

Shows the time estimates for all unresolved issues assigned to a user across projects. This helps you understand the user's workload better.

Version Workload Report

Shows the time estimates for all unresolved issues assigned to a version, broken down by user and issues. This helps you understand the remaining work for the version.

Summary

In this chapter, we covered how each phase of test management can be performed using the Test Management plugins in Jira. We also compared the features provided by each plugin. Requirements are the documented needs of the end user, which are captured in Jira using issue types. We learned to add and modify issue types and workflows for use in our projects in Jira. Test cases can be organized based on components or requirements using test suites. We saw how test suites can be created in Jira using the plugins. Planning is essential to manage the testing phase. The test plan enables us to strategize how tests will be executed. We compared how each plugin provides the test plan feature. Traceability reports help us backtrack defects to test cases and requirements. We explored how each plugin provides its version of traceability reports. Finally, we familiarized ourselves with the reports section in Jira, which will be covered in detail in Chapter 10, *Test Execution Status Reporting*.

In the next chapter, we'll look at the best approaches for selecting various project execution workflows, based on the project's needs.

Section 3: Test Management - Manage and Plan

Readers will learn how to plan and manage a workflow that suits their project's needs.

This section will include the following chapters:

- Chapter 4, *Test Management Approach*
- Chapter 5, *Test Planning*

Test Management Approach

4

Execution strategy in the test management approach plays a crucial role in determining the success or failure of the testing cycle. The strategy helps to identify optimized pathways to mitigate risks early. In this chapter, we will cover in detail the best approaches for selecting various project execution workflows based on the project's needs. We'll learn how to create ad hoc test runs and execute test cases in the test cycles as part of a test plan. Then, we'll understand the importance of each execution type, and its benefits and targeted purpose. Let's get started with the execution strategy for structured testing with **Test Management Approach (TMap)**.

In this chapter, we'll cover the following topics:

- Execution strategy for structured testing with TMap
- Execution in test cycles for selected release
- Best practices for test management

Execution strategy for structured testing with TMap

With the evolution of the software industry and their standards, the emphasis is for processes to be driven by business objectives, rather than processes being drivers of business objectives. This led to the creation of the following two ways of assessing the test process:

- **Prescriptive**: In this approach, the model provides a framework along with the **key performance indicators (KPIs)** and questions to ask for each test unit. This helps you identify the root causes of inefficiencies. It also provides the order in which each of these inefficiencies should be tackled to improve the process.

- **Non-prescriptive**: In this approach, the model provides a framework along with the KPIs and questions to ask for each test unit; it doesn't dictate the order to attack these issues. Instead, the organization needs to evaluate the business value derived from solving each problem, and first tackle the problems that offer the highest returns.

An example of the prescriptive approach is the **Test Maturity Model** (**TMM**), which complements the CMMI model. We'll be using a non-prescriptive approach, such as the TMap that was proposed by the Dutch division of testing practice at Sogeti. It's based on **business-driven test management** (**BDTM**), which emphasizes business priorities to drive testing efforts, utilizes a structured life cycle approach, and provides checklists and templates, while offering the flexibility to adapt to changes and situations. The latest version of TMap and TMap NEXT provides the following steps in its business-driven approach:

1. The test manager establishes and creates the test goal, which details the requirements, use cases, and change requests, along with the characteristics relevant to the client for each item being tested.
2. A master test plan risk table is created by the test manager, which assigns a risk class to each unit and characteristic being tested, along with the levels of testing, such as unit test, system test, and regression test.
3. Once the master test plan risk table is ready, the test manager determines the test intensity for each test unit based on the risk class. Test intensity ranges from light (•), medium (••), thorough (•••), to **Implicit** (**I**)— where characteristics, such as usability and responsiveness, being tested will be recorded as part of the execution of other test cases, or **static** (**S**)—using checklists instead of writing test cases. The output of this iterative step is the master test plan strategy table.
4. Based on the guidelines provided in the master test plan strategy table, we determine the depth of testing by test level. This is captured in the output, which is called the **test plan strategy table**. This table is used to estimate the cost of testing and helps to balance the testing efforts and risks identified.
5. Once the effort estimates are confirmed and the stakeholders are informed, the test design table is generated by utilizing the test specification techniques based on the test plan strategy table and test basis, that is, the requirements specification document. This table is later used to design actual test cases and scripts that will be executed in the test process. Execution of the tests can be broken down based on the efforts and its scope. The urgency to deliver specific tasks can help the team to decide the best approach to test and validate its functionality.

We will be covering each of the steps in the business-driven approach in the following chapters. For more details on the TMap approach, check out `http://www.tmap.net`. Checklists and other templates are also provided with example cases for download at `http://www.tmap.net/checklists-and-templates`.

Based on the aforementioned approach, the execution can follow either of the two following types of test strategies:

- Ad hoc test runs
- Execution in test cycles for selected releases

Let's look at these approaches in detail.

Ad hoc test runs

The testing team faces a variety of situations during the test process based on the maturity of the processes followed in the organization to deliver products on a schedule. The following are some examples of these situations:

- The turnaround window is short, such as in the following examples:
    - Testing for bug fixes after the product went live and needs to be fixed quickly
    - A small change request in the maintenance phase that needs to be handled quickly
- The workflows to validate is less complex, such as in the following examples:
    - Testing for requirements where the scope is minimum and requires less testing, such as adding validation popups to forms to prompt end users to fill in all fields
    - Cosmetic changes, such as changing the text on a button in the UI from **OK** to **Accept**

In these situations, the underlying factor is that the changes are not drastic and the scope of testing is very limited. Hence, in such situations, we can adopt the ad hoc testing approach.

The **ad hoc testing** procedure is a three-step process of understanding requirements, building test cases for the test requirements, and executing them as needed. In this approach, a test professional simply creates the least possible number of test cases, links them to the relevant requirements, and then performs test execution at the test case level. During test execution, testers can update the status of the execution supported with the required artifacts. This saves considerable overhead and time on arranging meetings, preparing test plans, test cycles, waiting to get sign-off for test plans, and so on.

Let's see how we can execute test cases as part of an ad hoc test run in the synapseRT, Zephyr, and Test Management tools.

synapseRT

Test cases can be executed as and when they're needed as part of an ad hoc execution. In synapseRT, you can create the test case as a Jira ticket. Since a test case is just another type of Jira ticket, it has default fields like any other issue types in the **Details** section. However, it does contain **Test Step**, **Automation**, and **Ad hoc Test Run** sections, as shown in the following screenshot:

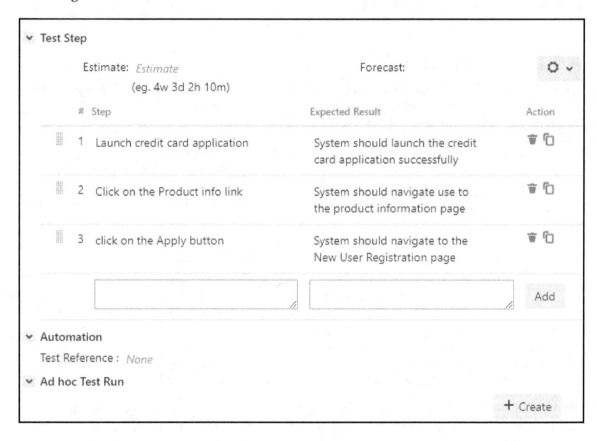

Now, on clicking the **Create** button, an ad hoc test run is created for the selected test case. Testers can execute each step and update the status of the execution, add a new defect or link an existing one, attach artifacts, and so on, as shown in the following screenshot:

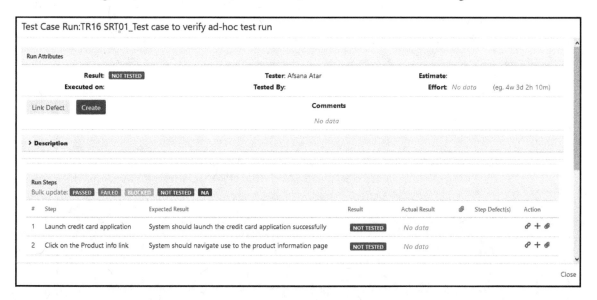

You can execute the selected test case multiple times and can have multiple ad hoc runs, as shown in the following screenshot, in the **Ad hoc Test Run** section:

Zephyr

Zephyr executes the test case as an ad hoc run or as a part of the ad hoc test cycle. In order to do so, the user just needs to create a test case issue type and enter all the required details. Once it's created, you can see the **Execute** button under the **Test Case Summary** field, as shown in the following screenshot:

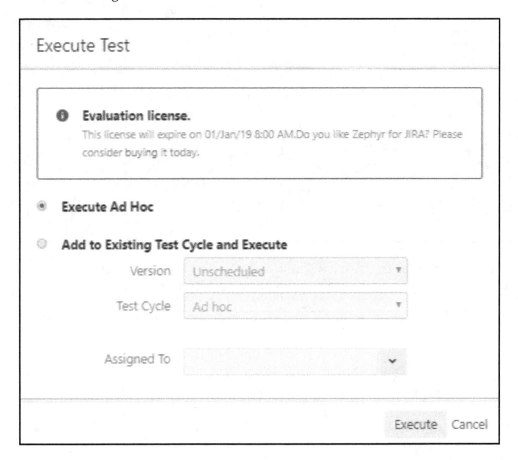

Alternatively, we can also create an ad hoc test cycle by navigating to **Tests** | **Cycle Summary** tab. It gives us an option to add or remove multiple test cases as part of an ad hoc test cycle:

After adding test cases to the ad hoc cycle, it looks like the following screenshot. As you can see, it gives us an option to organize the ad hoc test cycle as per your release. It also shows a detailed summary of the added test cases, including their ticket **ID**, **Summary**, current execution **Status**, and linked **Defects**:

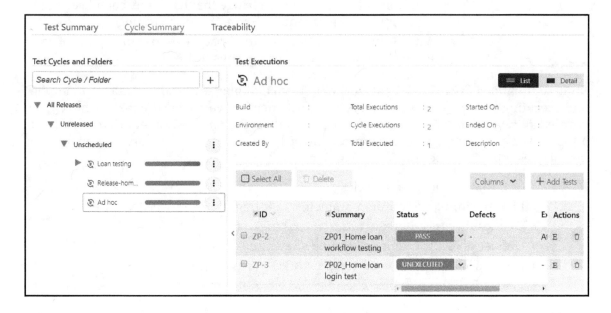

Test Management

The ad hoc test execution option is not supported by the Test Management tool. However, it does support the execution in a test cycle, which we will see in detail in the following section.

Execution in test cycles for selected releases

Ad hoc testing is a flexible and faster way to test shorter workflows. However, this approach isn't effective when you want to plan for the entire release or want to cover several testing types/characteristics, such as performance, security, acceptance, and integration. In such cases, we can consider preparing test cycles and then executing test cases as per the test strategy defined in the test plan. Let's consider some situations that a testing team faces when using the ad hoc approach:

- The turnaround time is longer, such as in the following examples:
    - The team is building a new project and is targeting the release of the product by the end of the year.
    - An upgrade of the product is planned to be released in this quarter.
- The workflow to validate has more steps and/or is complex, such as in the following examples:
    - A customer has requested a change that has large, complex requirements, and it requires more thorough testing.
    - When testing a reported bug to impact several components of an application, which requires rigorous testing.

In these situations, we need to analyze the problem and plan our testing strategy. Planning and executing test cases in cycles can be the most effective way to ensure that we have covered all types of required testing for the desired product or application. Hence, we adopt the *execution in the test cycle* approach, which gives us an opportunity to prepare a detailed test plan that does the following things:

- Calls out all the dependencies
- Lists the input and output parameters required to execute the test cases
- Defines success criteria in order to pass the test
- Defines defect tracking and testing strategies
- Designs and performs end-to-end workflows as per the use cases
- Plans for different types of testing and integrates them in terms of the test cycles

- Designs test cases for smoke, sanity, integration, cross browser, or even environment testing, and so on

Since the change is huge, as its impact, we are better prepared with the preceding approach. Let's see in detail how Jira plugins can be used to plan our executions in different types of cycles.

synapseRT

Test cycles are a part of the test plan ticket in synapseRT. Hence, in order to create test cycles, we need to create a test plan first. Once the test plan is ready, you can add the test cases or test suites, which can then be categorized under the test cycle based on their types, priority, or other execution criteria.

The following screenshot shows a test plan with three test cycles—Credit Card type A, Credit Card type B, and Regression Test:

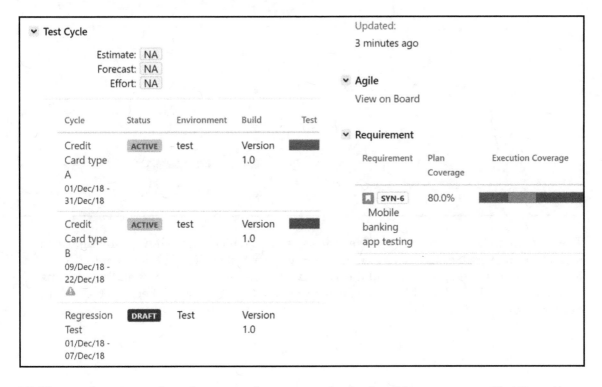

We'll cover how to track and execute these test cycles in detail in Chapter 7, *Test Execution Phase*.

Zephyr

On the other hand, if you want to create different types of test cycles based on the testing needs, Zephyr categorizes them under the **Cycle Summary** tab of the **Tests** section. The following image shows two main test cycles—Loan Testing and Ad hoc. Loan testing has the Education loan, Personal loan, Car loan, and Home loan subtest cycles:

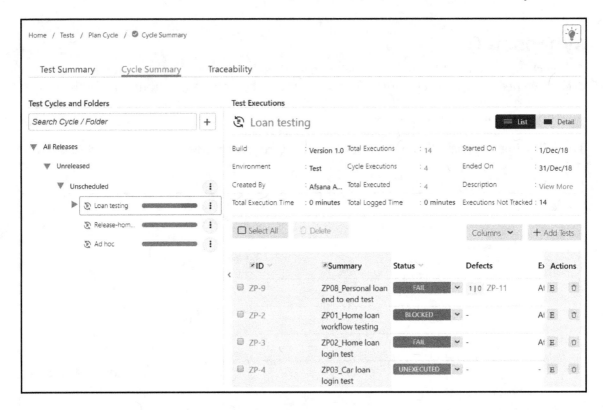

The test case ticket also has a **Test Executions** section, which shows how many times this test has been executed ad hoc or as a part of any other test cycles. As shown in the following screenshot, if we expand the **Test Executions** section, it shows all the test runs with the test cycle under which it has been executed. It also shows linked defects and the execution date:

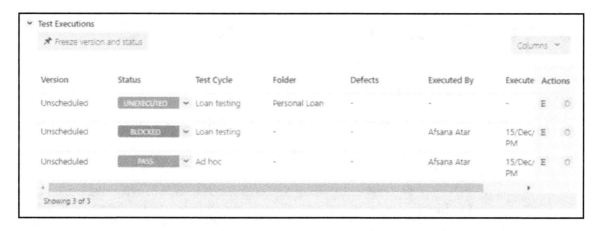

Test management

In the Test Management tool, test cycles can be created from the **Cycles** tab. As shown in the following screenshot, for a banking application, we have `Credit Score Release` as the main test cycle. Under this, we have three subtest cycles—`Acceptance Tests`, `Functional Tests`, and `Regression Tests`. Each cycle contains the required set of test cases, and their execution status can be viewed from the **Progress** column:

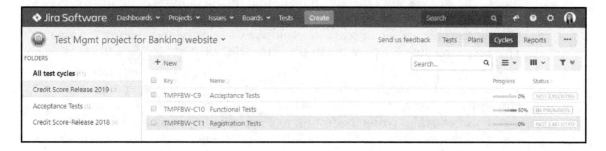

Best practices for test management

The TMap provides guidance for implementing a structured testing approach in an organization. Here are a few important factors that'll help you create a strong foundation to establish the test-management practice:

- Utilize a model for the testing activities based on the development process. In our case, we use the STLC model, which is a subset of the SDLC model for the testing activities. The TMap life cycle model can be used for the test management activities.

- Ensure that appropriate testing tools and techniques, such as checklists, are adopted to identify, execute, track, and communicate progress and results. Communication is essential to identify and tackle obstacles quickly and in time.

- Establish the required test environments with the infrastructure that meets both the software and hardware requirements to operationalize the product in the test. This also includes setting up a test database and test data. This will enable a smoother execution phase.

- For effective test management, the testing team should be a group with the right combination of testing skills and knowledge of the product. This also means that the organization should ensure the staff are trained and processes are improved so as to achieve the maturity levels necessary to establish a scalable and repeatable success story. Establishing a solid organization with mature processes ensures that the team follows common terminologies, approaches, tools, techniques, entry and exit criteria, weekly or daily calls, and reporting formats. This helps the top management in the generation of standard reporting artifacts.

- Automation is key and hence the organization must try to incorporate open source or paid testing tools that will help testers to perform their job more efficiently. Automating repetitive activities can help testers to focus on exploratory testing, while the testing tool performs regression testing. Before adopting these tools, a cost-to-benefit analysis should be performed, since such tools require considerable ramp-up time for training and gaining skills before staff can use them productively.

- Utilize the artifacts from each step of the BDTM process to ensure the test goals are clear and specific to the testing requirements. This helps in analyzing the test basis thoroughly, implementing strategies well in time, and achieving good test coverage.

- The aim of testing is to have a feasible test coverage over the functions and requirements of the product. The bigger the project, the greater the test levels and test units. Hence, it's essential to use test suites to organize them. Also, avoid merging and covering large complex requirements in one test case by adding a large number of test steps—instead, add them to separate test cases to verify the functionality more accurately.

Summary

In this chapter, we covered the best approaches for selecting various project execution strategies, as well as different approaches to execute test cases during the test execution phase. The TMap provides a structured approach for testing. We learned about the BDTM approach. For shorter and less complex requirements, the ad hoc test strategy can be used to effectively and efficiently test and validate the requirements. We learned how ad hoc testing can be implemented using the Jira plugins. Execution in test cycles is required to organize and manage test cases for bigger and more complex projects. We learned how test cycles can be created and organized using the Jira plugins. Finally, we discussed the best practices to establish a strong foundation for effective test management.

In the next chapter, we'll learn about different aspects of test planning and test strategies, while understanding the relationship between requirements and the test plan.

5
Test Planning

Test planning is the most essential stage in the STLC. Planning gives test professionals the opportunity to build an understanding of the problem in terms of the complexity of requirements. This is achieved by analyzing the workflow based on the use cases, and then deriving the test cases from it. A requirements document is the test basis that specifies the functionality of the application. The test plan then specifies how those items will be covered in the test by using several artifacts, including the test assignment, approach, and test strategy. The test strategy is a particularly important artifact of the test process.

We will cover different aspects of test planning and test strategy while understanding the relationship between the requirements and test plan. We will also look at how Jira can help us in defining and comparing strategies for our testing needs using synapseRT, Zephyr, and the Jira Test Management tool.

In this chapter, we will learn about the following topics:

- Creating and organizing a test plan using Jira plugins
- Defining and implementing the test strategy
- Establishing relations between requirements and the test plan

Creating and organizing a test plan using Jira plugins

There are various workflows involved in the test planning phase. If one is utilizing the TMap approach, the test planning phase corresponds to the planning and control phase in the TMap life cycle. The planning phase consists of creating the test strategy using product risk analysis, estimation, and planning, while the control phase aims for continuous quality improvement by monitoring, reporting, and adjusting to reach the test goals. Let's delve into learning the activities in the test planning phase.

Once the test assignment has been confirmed, the team starts discussions about the stated specifications during the planning meeting, where the team tries to break down vague and complex statements into logical and clear units that can be added to the product build and test process. The development and testing teams, along with business analysts, create a sample model or prototype of the web page or application that needs to be built. The requirements specification document, the functional document, and the prototype thus form the test basis—the baseline document for the testers.

Having achieved clarity regarding the test basis, the test manager initiates the preparation of the test plan. The test plan is a document that defines the planning and execution strategy for the selected project. It has the following sections:

Purpose or background	The reason or purpose of the project and the need for testing
Scope of the testing	This outlines all the agreed features or components that will be considered for testing as part of the test preparation or execution phase.
Out of scope	This lists all the components where testing is not required.
Resources	This section describes the currently allocated number of resources, their expertise and skill levels, as well as their roles and responsibilities.
Timeline	This section details the project schedule and the start and end times of the testing phase as well as the schedule for each test cycle/iteration if possible.
Dependency	If there are any dependencies without which the team cannot start testing, then it's always a good idea to list them under this section; for example, the build should be deployed in the correct environment before the testers can start testing.
Entry and exit criteria	This section highlights the test execution start and end criteria, based on which basis test results will be accepted.
Deliverables at the end of each phase	This lists the types of artifacts that will be generated, signed off, and added to the project repositories for reference.
Risks	This highlights the areas of the product or application where the chances of risk are high or low. Based on their impact, testers can design additional types of testing or test cases to mitigate them well in advance. Details of the **Product Risk Analysis** (**PRA**) are captured in this section.
Test strategy	Using the PRA and the test goal, the test strategy is established to ensure that appropriate test coverage will be achieved for all functions based on their risk levels/classes.

Tools and techniques	Depending on the testing strategy and project testing requirements, teams can opt for appropriate tools for test management, automation, for team collaboration, for creating a knowledge base, or even for comparing, validating, or analyzing the data. These tools include Jira, Confluence, Selenium, HP ALM, Jenkins, Visual Studio, Eclipse or Toad for Oracle, and Tableau.
Environment details	It's always a good idea to perform testing for each level in a separate environment. Hence, depending on the types of testing, testers can have test environments, such as beta or UAT environments, or automation environments, which would be separate from production and development environments.
Test data requirements	Testing requires a set of input data in order to validate the accuracy of the planned workflows and the outcome it generates by following that workflow. Sometimes, test data preparation is done by a different team and, hence, it creates a dependency, or there might be a dependency on running certain types of jobs that generates the required data. In such cases, the testers are required to document such dependencies in the test plan, as well as in the test cases.
Requirement document details	The test basis or baseline document may consist of documents such as the use case document, layout and design documents, the requirement specification document, data flow documents, and technical design documents. These documents give a clear understanding of the components or features in detail. It's good practice to add links to these documents in the test plan.
Closure and approvals	This section specifies the conditions based on which we can mark the test as completed to close the phase or cycle. It also lists the documents required to be produced as a part of the closure process, as well as a list of approvals and approvers who will be signing off the documents, including the test plan.

Approaches to test plan preparation vary across different organizations. However, the thought process is the same. Some organizations emphasize the creation of a proper test plan document using the standard template, while others prefer creating and managing it in project management tools, while describing all the necessary details. You can visit the following link to download the template for a test plan based on the TMap approach: `http://www.tmap.net/building-blocks/test-plan`.

Now that we know what the test plan consists of, it's time to create one using Jira. Let's look at how we can use Jira to help us create and organize our test plans with the use of Jira plugins.

synapseRT

A test plan in synapseRT is nothing but another issue type. Once we create a test plan ticket, it's time to add details, such as priority, descriptions, and current status. After that, we can either create a new test case or add test suites with the desired test cases. Furthermore, we can also create test cycles to segregate these test cases and make them part of a selected cycle:

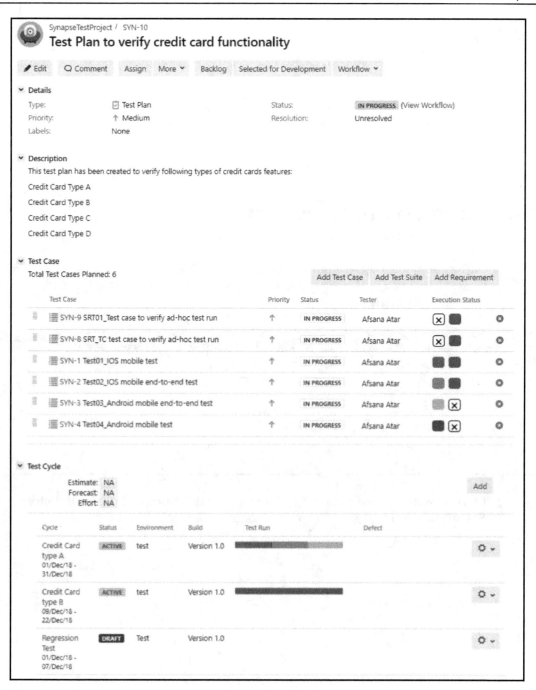

Creating a test plan using synapseRT

Zephyr

The test plan option is available with Zephyr Enterprise version only, where the user can create and manage test plans using test cycles.

Please feel free to explore the Zephyr Enterprise version from this link: `https://zephyrdocs.atlassian.net/wiki/spaces/ZE6/pages/149455000/Test+Planning`.

The Test Management tool

In order to create a test plan in the Test Management tool, we need to follow these steps:

1. Navigate to the **Tests** | **Plans** section. Click on the **+New** button to create a new plan. There is an option on the left-hand side panel to create multiple folders and organize test plans under main or subfolders:

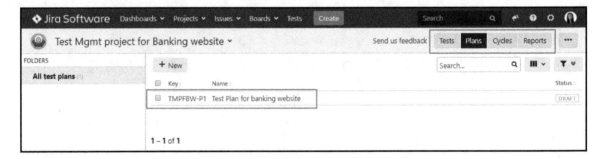

2. Once we add the test plan with some basic details such as **Name**, **Objective**, **Status**, or **Owner**, then we can move onto the **Traceability** tab:

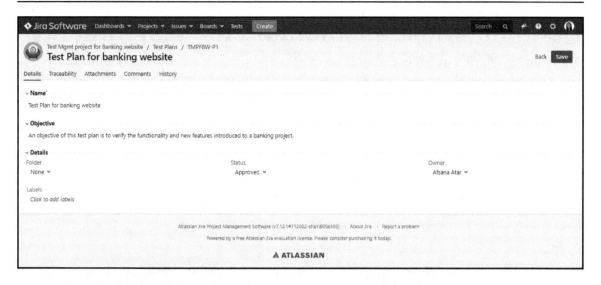

3. Under the **Traceability** option, we can search for the existing test cycles and select one or multiple test cycles to add them to a test plan. While searching for existing test cycles, it also shows the execution status of each test cycle with the owner's details, date, and the defects identified:

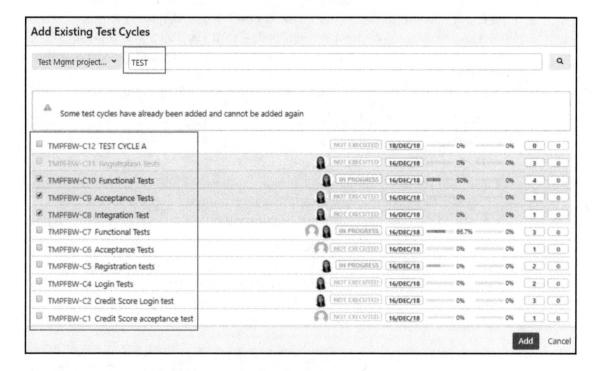

Defining and implementing the test strategy

Your test strategy completely depends on the testing needs of an application; primarily, the risk class of each requirement. For example, if the requirement is to verify whether an application can process requests from 1,000 users accessing the application concurrently, then we need to add performance testing to our testing strategy. We can perform stress testing by discovering the breakpoint above the permitted threshold as a part of our test strategy. We can also perform load testing by analyzing the performance of the application based on the permissible user limits hitting the application concurrently. We can also measure the response time of an application in order to render all the page components/objects with the different load ranges.

Let's understand the process of creating a test strategy to test a banking application. This is a four step process:

1. Map characteristics such as functionality and usability, as we saw in `Chapter 1`, *An Overview of Software Quality Assurance*, with the use cases from the test basis or the test goals table, if available.

2. Based on this, an appropriate risk class is assigned to each use case. The levels of risk can vary based on the standards set in your organization. In our example, we consider risk levels A (highest) to I (lowest), with 3 levels in each sub-risk level of high (A, B, and C), medium (D, E, and F), and low (G, H, and I).

3. We have also decided on the five test levels—**unit test (UT)**, **system test (ST)**, **user acceptance test (UAT)**, **pre-production test (Pre-PT)**, and **post production test (Post-PT)**.

4. Now, based on the risk class, we can define appropriate test intensities as:

   - **Light**: It is signified by (•)
   - **Medium**: It is signified by (••)
   - **Thorough**: It is signified by (•••)
   - **Implicit (I)**: It has characteristics such as usability and responsiveness being tested will be recorded as part of the execution of other test cases
   - **Static (S)**: It uses checklists instead of writing test cases which are assigned to each use case

Now, while assigning these test intensities, care must be taken that use cases with high risks have at least one test level that covers the tests thoroughly (•••), while use cases with medium risks need at least one test level with medium (••) coverage.

As per the TMap approach, the aim of this step is to create a test strategy table. Let's see an example test strategy table for testing the banking application:

Characteristics/Use case (UC)	Risk class	UT	ST	UAT	Pre-PT	Post-PT
Functionality						
UC.1.1 – All the modules for credit cards, home loans and personal banking sections function as expected.	A	•	•••	••	•	•
UC.1.2 – Account holders can apply for home loans and credit cards.	B	•	•••	•	•	•
UC.1.3 – Users cannot open multiple accounts for the same module.	C	•	•••	•	•	•
Performance						
UC.1.4 – For all website modules, all the components of the pages should be rendered within 30 seconds.	C	•	•••	••	•	•
UC.1.2 – The website should work fine under the threshold limit of 10,000 users accessing the application concurrently.	A		•••	••		•
Compatibility						
UC.2.1 – The application should work fine on different types of operating system, such as Windows, and Linux.	B	•	•••	••	•	•
UC.2.2 – The mobile app should work fine on different operating systems, such as Windows, iOS, and Android.	B	•	•••	••	•	•
UC.1.4 – The application should work with third-party credit score applications.	D	•	••	•		•
Usability						
UC.3.5 – All the text on the UI should be clear, visible, and have help text for users to use.	E		••	•	•	
UC.1.5 – Every section should be reachable within three clicks, and the user should be able to navigate to their desired page.	G	I	I			
UC.3.2.1 – All warning and error messages should be highlighted in specified colors (warning: yellow, error: red).	H	•	I			
Localization						

UC.3.1 – Users should be able to view the page content in supported languages, such as Chinese, Japanese, French, Spanish, and English.	B	•	•••	••		•	•
UC.3.2 – All text should be translated correctly, including the warning and error messages.	H	•	•	•		•	•
UC.3.3 – The functionality of the application should remain the same in all the supported languages.	A	•	•••	••		•	•

Once this is established, there are various testing types or techniques to perform tests based on the required test intensity. Let's see a few examples of the types of testing that can be employed for our banking application:

- **Functional testing**: In order to ensure that the designed website serves the purpose, functional testing is performed, which covers all the positive, negative, smoke, and sanity test cases, where we check whether the functionality adheres requirements.

- **UI testing**: If the application is expected to face many users, then it is of the utmost importance to pay attention to every single UI element, feature, and function listed on the web page. This consists of verification of buttons, links, texts, warning messages, text alignment, look and feel, and so on.

- **Integration testing**: A banking application is constituted of different pages, modules, and components. Hence, it's important to check whether the final integrated product works smoothly. It's important to check the data flow and accuracy in such cases. For example, in the case of the banking application, it consists of a personal account section, a loan section, an insurance section, credit card sections, and so on. Now, in this instance, it's important to verify the workflow where current account holders can view the credit card offers and be able to apply for them without opening a new account separately.

- **Compatibility testing**: It is important to test whether the application is compatible with different environments, including different operating systems, databases, and devices. It is also important to check whether the application integrates smoothly with other supported vendor products and gives results as expected.

- **Browser testing**: If the application is supported by various browsers, testers should consider testing the web application in different browsers with the supported version of the browsers.

- **Localization testing**: If the application is being launched in different countries and in local languages, then there is a need for localization testing. You should verify the translation of words from English to the selected language, along with the application's behavior.

- **Exploratory testing**: In order to identify any hidden defects, exploratory testing is a useful tool. It simply randomly verifies any features, workflows, or any part of the application. It can be at a high or low level, as chosen by the testers.
- **Performance testing**: It is useful to check the performance of the application, since it will be open to access by a large audience. Hence, you should test whether the application can withstand a huge load. Performance testing contains stress and load testing.

Apart from these techniques, if needed, you can always incorporate other types in the testing strategy based on your project requirements.

Establishing relations between requirements and the test plan

As we saw in `Chapter 3`, *Understanding Components of Testing with Jira*, the traceability matrix is useful for obtaining a clear understanding of the project progress and identify requirements that demand more testing efforts or have more defects. The traceability matrix also indicates the test strategy, the type of test activity, and the tasks that have been defined and planned by test professionals to verify stated requirements. This gets created early in the phase so that it can be reviewed by project stakeholders, which affords sufficient time to monitor it, provide feedback, and adjust the test process as required by the team to achieve the test goal.

Establishing relations between the requirements and the test plan is the first part of creating the traceability matrix. Whenever a requirement ticket is created in Jira, test professionals can prepare a test plan ticket and link it to the requirement. One requirement may have a master test plan, and/or multiple sub-test plans, depending on testing requirements. This gives an opportunity to project managers to track the test planning details for the selected requirement. These requirements can vary from an Epic or Story with a targeted release deadline, to any bugs reported by customers that require huge amounts of testing.

Let's understand how we can establish the relationship between the requirements and the test plan using Jira plugins.

synapseRT

It's easy to establish a relationship between a requirement and test plan using the test cases. While creating a test plan in the preceding section, we saw how we can add test cases to our test plan. In the same way, you can add the same test cases to the requirement ticket as well. The following screenshot depicts a **Story** issue type, with the four test cases added to it under the **Test Cases** section:

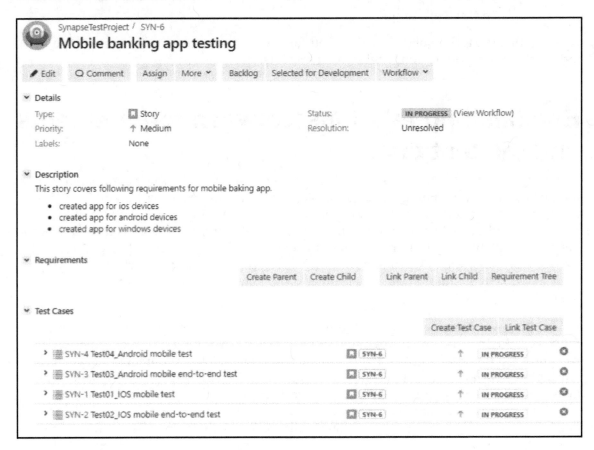

Once we add the same test cases to the test plan, we can see requirement coverage under the **Requirement** section, as shown in the following screenshot. This indicates that, in order to verify the requirement, the tester has added four test cases and all of them have been considered in this test plan. Hence, the requirement coverage percentage is **100.0%**.

Zephyr

As the test plan feature is only available in Zephyr Enterprise, we can link the test cases to the requirements in order to establish a relationship between them. As shown in the following screenshot, open the existing test case and navigate to the **More Actions** | **Link** option. Then, search for the relevant requirement issue ticket and link it, shown as follows:

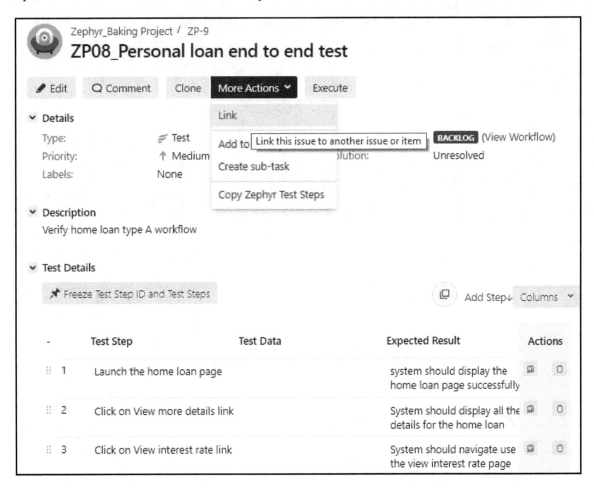

The Test Management tool

In the case of the Test Management tool, go to **Tests** | **Plan** and select the test plan for which you want to add the requirement. Then, go to the **Traceability** section, where you can search for existing user stories or requirements and link them to the test plan as follows:

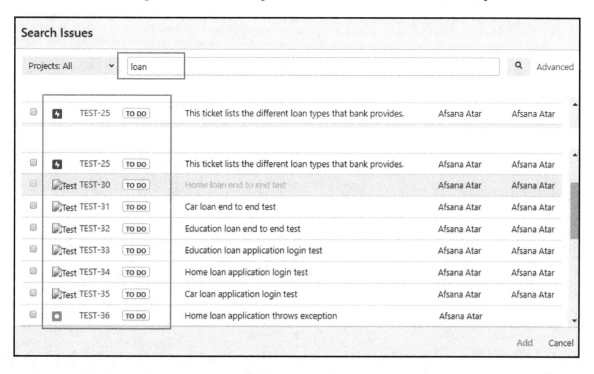

As you can see in the following screenshot, the **Issues** section shows the relevant requirements for which this test plan has been created, along with the test cycles that need to be executed in order to complete the verification process:

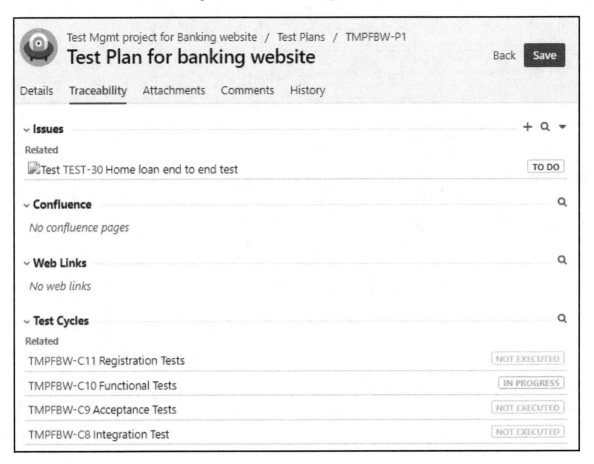

Summary

In this chapter, we covered different aspects of test planning and test strategy, while learning about the relationship between the requirements and the test plan. We understood the components of a general test plan that can be used during the test planning process. We also learned how to write test plans using Jira plugins.

There are various ways to define a test strategy. We looked at an example of creating a test strategy for a banking application using the TMap approach. In order to create a traceability matrix, we need to establish a relationship between test cases and test plans, and the test requirements. In this chapter, we saw precisely how we can link test plans to their related requirements.

In the next chapter, we will learn about the process of test case design and creation. We will also learn about organizing test cases, and hone our skills in reusing test cases and test data.

Section 4: Test Management - Design and Execute

We will learn in detail about the best approaches to selecting from various project execution workflows based on a project's needs, learning different aspects of test design, test strategy, and test execution.

This section will include the following chapters:

- Chapter 6, *Test Design Phase*
- Chapter 7, *Test Execution Phase*
- Chapter 8, *Defect Management Phase*

6
Test Design Phase

A test case can be defined as a set of instructions for a user (tester) so that they can perform tests on an application in a predefined state. They will also need the predefined set of test data to get the expected results that are mentioned in the requirements. Testing cannot be done without a test case, as the product verification process starts with these test cases. They can either be automated or manual, but the objective remains the same.

In this chapter, we will cover the following topics, as well as learn about the test design phase in detail:

- Creating and maintaining test cases
- Reusing test cases and test data
- Organizing test cases

Creating test cases

After the test team understands the requirements of the project, the test plan is prepared and approved. Now, the test team can start the **test design phase**—this phase requires the test team to create the test scenarios and test cases. In cases where automation testing is involved, a testable version of the product becomes available, which leads to the creation of the test scripts as well.

The test case should briefly describe the purpose of the test, user actions, and the expected results as a result of those actions. The following are the details that are added while creating a test case:

Test Case Field	Description
TC-ID	A test case ID helps you identify test cases uniquely. Usually, it is added by the testing tools. However, testers can also add a unique ID to segregate test cases from one another in test suites.
Title	This includes the title of the test case, which describes the test's purpose.

Test Suite	Identifying test cases as a part of the selected test suite helps test professionals to manage them at the time of creation.
Actions	This section consists of the actions that testers need to perform in order to verify the functionality of the project.
Expected Results	These describe the results of the activity performed by the testers in the actions section.
Test Data	This specifies the set of input conditions or parameters that are needed to execute a test case or a state of the application from where test case execution can begin.
Priority	A priority of a test case can either be critical, high, medium, or low, depending on the functionality for which it has been designed.
Requirement ID	This involves linking a requirement to a test case for which it has been designed.
Date of Creation	This means the date when the test case was designed. Testing tools usually add the dates automatically.
Environment	Defining the environment is required to understand which environment a test has been designed for, for example, a test environment, UAT, post-production, and so on.
Preconditions	This frames the conditions that need to be satisfied before the test execution begins. For example, an application should be up and running, the required build version should be deployed, the user should have access to the application with the specified role, and so on.
Build Number	It's useful to know which build version this testing is being designed for. It becomes easy to track and debug the application for the specified build version, especially if it fails.
Release Number	When the test case is up for a release, it's a good idea to mention the release details in the test case. This makes it easy to group the test cases based on the release version of the application.
Project Name	This includes the project name for which the test case has been designed. It's a good practice to segregate test cases and group them by project name as it smoothens the maintainability of test cases.
Test Cycle Name	Test cycles specify the iteration that a test case is going to be a part of. It narrows down segregation further and helps identify test coverage easily.
Status	This field is used to mark the current status of the test case so that it is easy for the testers to take an action on it. During the test design phase, test cases can have the following status types such as, draft, ready for review, review completed, not executed, review pending, in progress.

Comments	It's often recommended to add comments whenever it's necessary so that if the test case is shared across the team, it's easy for them to be aware of certain situations before executing, reviewing, or modifying the test case. Comments also aid in easy handover and sharing of work within your team.

Organizations often have a customized set of fields for test cases, and so you might observe various formats for the preceding test case fields.

Prioritizing test cases

There are various methods for organizing test cases. You can add a label, project name, the requirement's details, or even test suite details to group them under a single branch. An example of this is the **test priority**. The test priority is an effective way of organizing the test cases. Test priority sets the importance for the selected test case to verify the stated functionality by defining the level of urgency that dictates the order of execution. The priority status is usually one of the following:

- **Critical**: These need to be added to the project verification iterations and need to be executed at the beginning of the iteration. Designing and executing the critical test cases helps in reducing product risks.
- **High**: These are important for the requirement verification process. After verifying critical priority test cases, the test team moves on to the high priority test cases.
- **Medium**: These include features worth validating; however, their impact is medium. Hence, during a tight execution schedule, the team cherry—picks a handful of test cases that will be the most relevant from the list for execution.
- **Low**: These have a minimal impact on the functionality of the application and are mostly designed to verify cosmetic changes in the application.

Test case status

The test case status during the test designing phase signifies the current state of the test case. Therefore, it's helpful for the team to take an action based on it. The test status during the test design phase can vary and be any of the following:

- **Draft/In Progress**: As the name suggests, when the test case is still under the designing phase and is incomplete, its status is marked as **Draft**.

- **Ready for Review**: Once the tester has finished adding the details in the test case and it's good to undergo review, the status can be set as **Ready for Review**.
- **Review Completed**: Once the test case has been peer reviewed, its status can be updated as **Review Completed**.
- **Ready/Not Executed/No Run**: The test case can be marked as **Ready** to be executed after it has been reviewed and modified, as per the review comments, and updated with the required test data. Some test management tools also have their status as **Not Executed** or **No Run** instead of **Ready**; however, the meaning remains the same.

Managing test artifacts and their formats

Test cases can be written and captured in a variety of formats, such as being stored in text files, Word documents, Excel workbooks, or by utilizing specialized test capture tools. The most prevalent way, however, is creating test cases in Excel sheets and loading them into the test management tools such as HP ALM, Jira and so on.

Apart from the detailed test execution steps, a test case can also have a variety of support documents or artifacts attached, such as the following:

- A prototype document that testers want to refer to during the execution phase
- User credentials
- A set of SQL queries and/or procedures that are needed for test execution
- Details regarding the scheduled jobs
- Links to documents that can be referred to during execution

Additionally, if the same test case has been utilized for one or more releases, then it can contain the execution artifacts, such as log files or screenshots that were generated during the previous release test. It is quite helpful to refer to the previously attached artifacts and compare the results of the current execution.

Let's see how we can create test cases and add the relevant details to them using the Jira tool.

synapseRT

To create a test case in synapseRT, test professionals need to follow these steps:

1. Select the **Test Case** option from the **Issue Type** field. The default issue type is **Story**; change it to **Test Case** and select the relevant project.
2. After selecting the issue type, it's time to enter all of the other required details, such as **Summary**, **Description**, **Priority**, **Labels**, **Assignee**, and **Epic link**. Once you are ready to create the test case, click on the **Create** button. We can always configure the fields that we want to display on this page using the **Configure Fields** icon from the top-right corner in the Jira issue:

3. Jira will successfully create a test case. As you can see in the following screenshot, the issue type is **Test Case**. After creating the test case, it's time to add other details, such as **Test Step** and **Expected Result**, and link a **Test Suite** and **Requirement** as applicable. As shown in the following screenshot, on the right-hand side, in the **Requirement** section, we can see that this test case has a relevant linked requirement and that it's part of RESET PASSWORD TESTS, which is a subtest suite under the CAR LOAN TYPE A TESTING **Test Suite**:

Zephyr

Zephyr also identifies a test case as another issue type. To create a test case in Zephyr, we need to follow these steps:

1. Select the issue type as **Test**. We also need to enter the other required details such as **Summary**, **Description**, **Priority**, **Linked Issues**, **Assignee**, **Test Step** with **Expected Result**, and **Test Data**. Click on the **Create** button to create the test case:

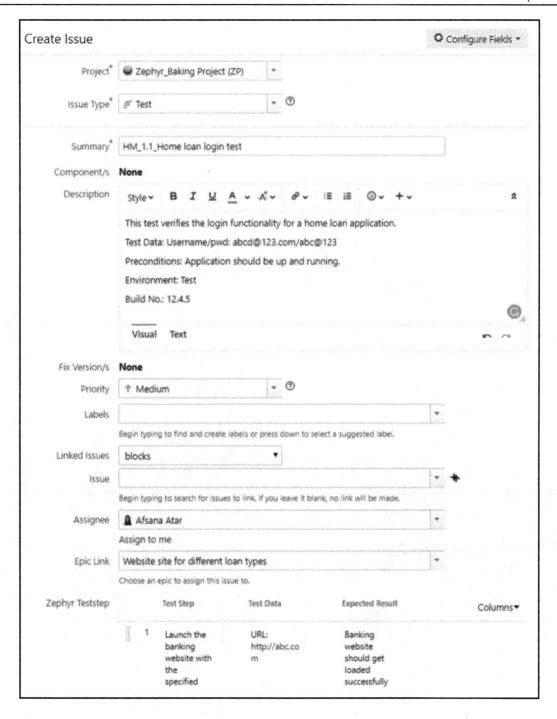

2. After creating the test case, you will see that it has all the details that we have entered. Like any Jira ticket, we can always modify these details. We also have the option to **Clone** the test case, add more related issues or requirements, or even start executing by clicking the **Execute** button:

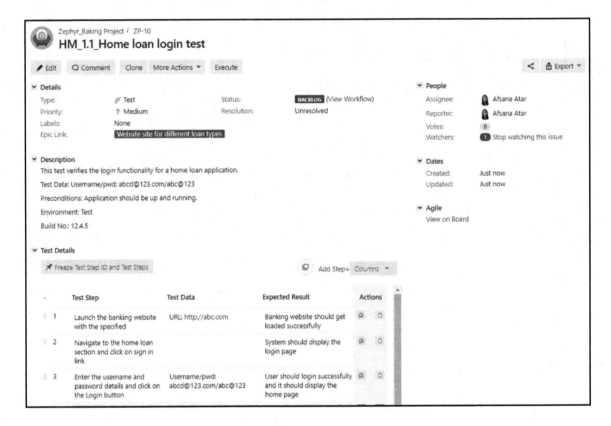

Test Management

To create a test case in the Test Management tool, we need to follow these steps:

1. First, navigate to the **Tests** section from the main tab and then click on the **+New** button to add a new test case. Now, we need to add a new test case under the `Test Mgmt project for Banking website` project:

2. After clicking on the **+New** button, enter the required details in the **Details** tab, such as the **Name** of the test case, **Objective**, **Preconditions** (if any), and other relevant details such as **Label**, **Status**, **Priority**, **Owner**, and so on.

3. Now, it's time to add the test steps. Click on the **Test Script** tab to add **STEP**, **EXPECTED RESULT**, and relevant **TEST DATA** details, as shown in the following screenshot. Once everything looks good, click on the **Save** button to save the changes to the test case:

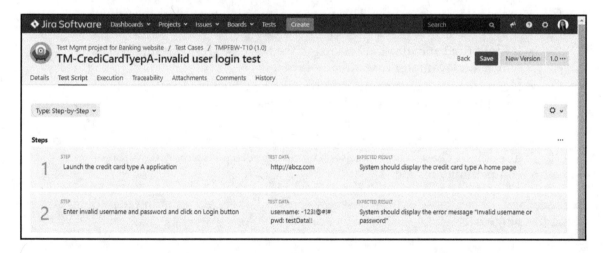

Reusing test cases across different projects

Now that we have learned how to write new test cases, let's look at how we can efficiently reuse existing ones for the project.

For a completely new project or release that doesn't have any dependent or related artifacts from past projects or releases, the test team must design all the test cases for all of the feature requests being released. However, as the product evolves and undergoes multiple releases, some of the common untouched features remain stable. This makes way for an opportunity to reuse test cases for future releases.

There are various reasons why you would want to reuse existing test cases:

- If you have a new team member joining the team, the existing test cases can help them familiarize with the product by going through the existing test cases.
- It reduces the overhead of creating all the test cases for the unchanged and already verified functionality from the previous releases. Testers can simply pull the existing valid test cases as part of the current iteration.
- It provides a baseline with the attached artifacts for testers to compare the functionality of the application.
- It helps to find missing functionality by comparing the execution results from previous releases.
- It helps in regression testing and verifying those parts of the application that haven't changed in the targeted release.
- It helps the team to be aware of any existing reported defects that could be linked to the relevant test cases. This provides direction for testers to verify the functionality that broke during the last release.
- It saves time and effort in reviewing the test cases for the same functionality for which a relevant test case already exists.
- It can also help other teams that are a part of the larger project to learn more about the previously released product or service when they want to refer to the existing test cases.
- If a new project has been introduced as an extension of the previous product, existing test cases can be reused by the team to perform integration or compatibility testing.

Let's see how we can reuse existing test cases and link them across multiple projects by using Jira plugins.

synapseRT

We can reuse existing test cases in synapseRT by adding them to the test suites under a different project. As shown in the following screenshot, the test cases SYN-1, SYN-3, and SYN-4 are part of SynapseTestProject, and have been added to a Reusing Existing Test Cases test suite, which is a part of the Banking payment using mobile devices project:

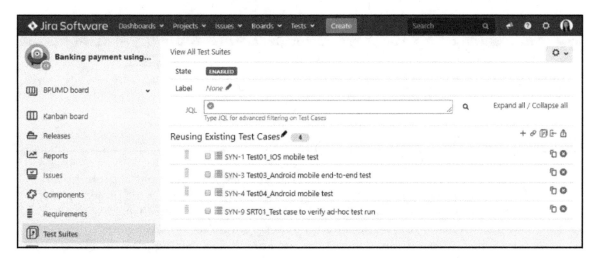

Zephyr

Zephyr doesn't support the functionality to copy the test cases or test cycles from one project to another. However, to reuse the existing test cases in another project, you can copy the structure of the test case, which only clones the issue structure.

If you want to explore this option, feel free to refer to the following page: https://wiki.almworks.com/display/structure/Copying+a+Structure.

Test Management

Test cases can be copied to another project in the Test Management tool so that they can be reused. To add them to a new project, we need to follow these steps:

1. Navigate to the **Test** tab and click on the ellipses. Select the option to **Import from other projects...**. As shown in the following screenshot, we are adding test cases to a new project, the `TM Mobile payment project`:

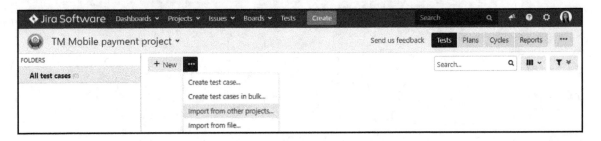

2. Now, from the **Projects** drop-down menu, select the name of the project from which you want to copy the test cases. As soon as you select the project name, it shows the test cases that exist under that project. Select the checkbox for all of the test cases that you want to add in your current project and drag and drop them into the left-hand side section. Once you are done selecting the relevant test case(s), click on the **Next** button. You will be shown the option to keep the links of these test cases to other issues and test attachments as is, as well as the option to map any test data to them:

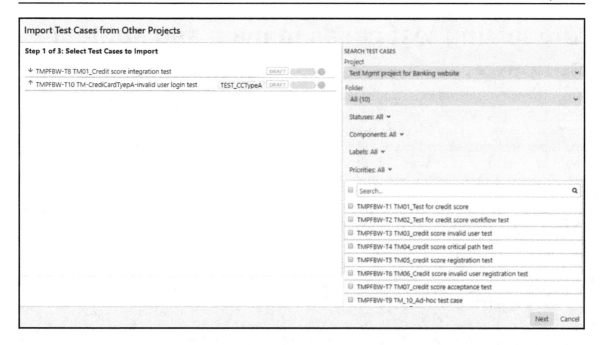

3. After selecting the appropriate options, you will be taken to the **Tests | All Test Cases** section. As shown in the following screenshot, two test cases have been added to our current project with a status of **DRAFT**:

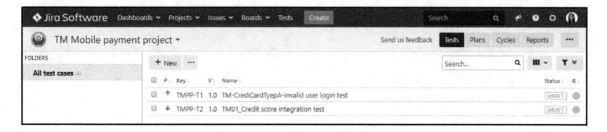

Organizing test cases in main and subtest suites

There are various factors that you need to consider while creating the main test suite and subtest suites to organize test cases. The main test suites can be created based on the project name or the module, and adding subtest suites helps to further categorize them based on the types of testing, environment, user role, and so on. As described in the test creation table, we can use one or more fields to categorize them, such as by project name, requirement ID, test verification environments, build number, or testing types.

 It's a good practice to add test cases as and when you create them, instead of sorting them out in bulk.

Jira plugins also provide us with the flexibility to organize test cases based on our criteria. Let's look at this in detail now.

synapseRT

Test cases pertaining to a project can be viewed from the **Test Suites** tab. As shown in the following screenshot, we can see all of the active test suites for a `SynapseTestProject` project in the active section of the **Test Suites** tab. We do have an option to **Clone** the test cases across different test suites in the same project:

To view all subtest suites and test cases, click on the edit icon for that test suite. As shown in the following screenshot, we have a test suite view in edit mode. It has two subtest suites with a total of four test cases:

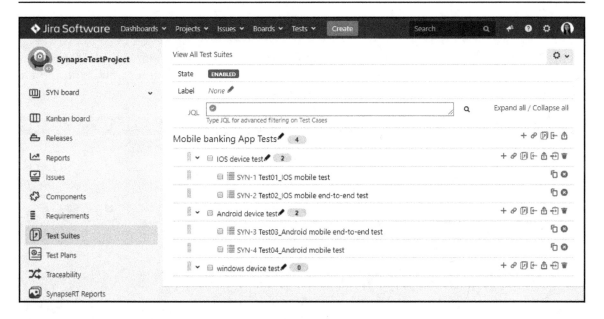

Zephyr

In Zephyr, all the test cases of the current projects are organized into separate cycles and sub-cycles under the **Tests** tab. As shown in the following screenshot, we can view the number of test cases and their current execution status by selecting the test cycle:

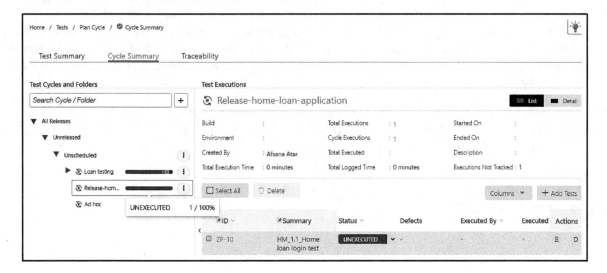

Test Management

In the Test Management tool, all of the test cases can be organized under the **Tests** tab. The following screenshot shows all the test cases under the **All test cases** folder, which can then be further organized under main and sub test suites:

Summary

In this chapter, we learned about the test design phase by creating and organizing test cases for a current project, as well as reusing them under a different project. A test case describes the step-by-step actions that a tester needs to perform to get their expected results. Setting up the current data or appropriate environment is essential for getting accurate results, since any change to the environment and test data can alter these results. Reusing these test cases across different projects as and when needed minimizes the time and effort spent on creating and reviewing test cases.

We saw how test cases can be reused across projects using Jira plugins. There are various ways to organize test cases in the test repositories. We can segregate them based on test suites, sub-test suites, label, requirement ID, and so on. We saw how Jira plugins can be used to create these test repositories for the project.

In the next chapter, we will take a closer look at the test execution phase and how this will be managed using Jira.

7
Test Execution Phase

Now that we understand what the test design phase is, it's time to move on to the next phase, that is, the test execution phase. This is a phase in the software testing life cycle where the build code is validated using the test cases that were designed and created in the test design phase.

While the development team is busy building the code for the application, the test team gears up the test design and test cycle preparation phases. It also utilizes this time to prepare test environments and test data. The team then starts the execution of the test cases, but only after the latest code changes have been deployed in the test environment or when the first testable components have been deployed for testing. Once the test environment is ready for testing, the test team performs a pretest to see whether the components are complete with respect to the expected functionality and thus are testable.

In this chapter, we will cover the following topics:

- Defining test cycles
- Adding test cases to test cycles from the same project
- Adding test cases to test cycles from different projects

We will also explain the process of test execution and how it will be managed using Jira.

Defining test cycles

Test cycles are designed based on the type of project the test team is working on. While designing test cycles, the test team performs the following tasks:

1. **Validates the test coverage**: This ensures that the test execution phase includes all of the test cases that are required to validate all of the requirements.

2. **Estimates the efforts**: Based on the complexity of the requirements, the priority of the test cases, the current skill level of the assigned resources, the availability of the testing tools, and the scope and allotted time, the test team estimates the time required to complete the test execution.

3. **Defines iterations**: If several defects are found during the initial test execution iteration, which results in a huge impact on the features of the application, the test team can always add another test execution iteration. Depending on the number of cycles, the buffer time, the defect retest time, and scheduled meetings, the estimation of test execution may vary.

There are various types of test cycles/iterations that the test team can design based on defined and implied customer needs. A few test cases should be designed as part of the smoke and regression test cycles as well:

- **Smoke test cycle**: This cycle enables testers to check whether the current deployed version is testable or not after the execution of a small set of test cases. For example, in the case of a banking website, some basic tests, such as launching the application, navigating through various tabs, clicking on the available links, and logging in and out of the application, can be helpful so that you can find out whether the application is working. If it breaks immediately after being launched or after clicking on the personal banking link, the team can report a defect. Then, the developers can start working on a fix right away. Smoke testing helps to ensure that the correct version of the build has been deployed in the requested test environment. Sometimes, during the deployment phase, the build can fail and developers might have to roll back the changes and redeploy the new build. In such cases, smoke testing is useful, as it can identify whether all the basic features are available to test and that no files or functionality are missing from the currently deployed build.

- **Regression test cycle**: This cycle is used to identify any adverse effects of the newly added/implemented requirements on the existing, workable solutions of the product or application. We can also use automated tools to schedule a regression test and gather the results as and when needed.

In `Chapter 4`, *Test Management Approach*, we looked at how we can add test cycles to a test plan. In the next section, we'll take a closer look at how to add and remove test cases from a test cycle, as well as how to start, complete, and abort test cycles in the test execution phase.

Adding test cases to the test cycle from the same project

Since we have already worked on the necessary test cases, they are ready to use and we can add them to a test cycle. Adding test cases from the current project is done by dragging and dropping or linking the test cases into the newly created test cycles. Let's look at how we can create and initialize test cycles. Once we have created test cycles, we can add test cases to them, update test cycles, and then commence with the test execution phase.

Initializing test cycles

Test cases are grouped to form test cycles or test iterations. Before we commence the execution of a cycle, it's important to check whether we have added the complete set of test cases that are required to verify a feature request. You should check the following before initializing a test cycle:

- The current build version that the testing will be performed against
- The test environment where the testing will be performed
- The execution start and end date
- The test cases should be organized based on their priority
- The test cases should be assigned to testers who will be responsible for executing the test cases

Let's look at how we can create and execute test cycles using Jira plugins.

synapseRT

In synapseRT, once test plan has been created and is ready, as it has had the test cases added to it, we can create test cycles:

1. Click on the **Add** button in the **Test Cycle** section and enter the test cycle details, such as **Name**, **Environment**, and **Start Date** and **End Date**, as shown in the following screenshot:

2. After creating the cycle, we have the option to change its state from **Draft** to **Start**, **Complete**, or **Abort**. We can also view and edit its details. To modify its details, click on **Edit** next to the newly created test cycle, as shown in the following screenshot:

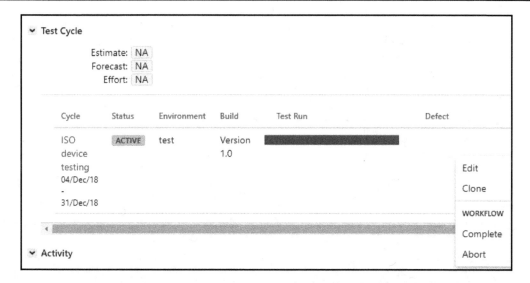

3. After adding the test cycle, we can see all of the test cases that have been added to the test plan as part of this test cycle. When the test cycle is in **DRAFT** state, we can add or remove test cases as needed. Once we start the test cycle, we cannot remove it, but we can always add test cases to it:

4. Once we commence the test cycle, we can start executing test cases. In synapseRT, we have the option to update the test execution status on the test step level, as well as on the test case level. As you can see in the following screenshot, the **Passed**, **Failed**, **Blocked**, **Not Tested**, and **NA** statuses are available for any test case:

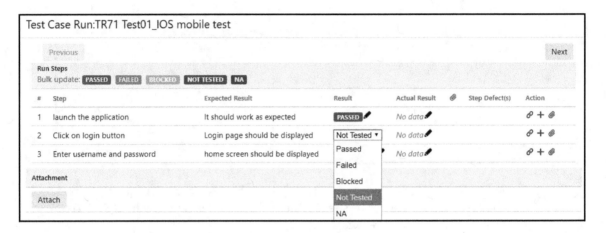

Zephyr

Like synapseRT, Zephyr doesn't need a test plan or test cases to create a test cycle. Follow these steps to create a test cycle:

1. When creating a test cycle in Zephyr, we can be more specific about its details, such as the **Version**, **Description**, **Name**, start and end dates, and so on. These details help us differentiate test cycles from one another:

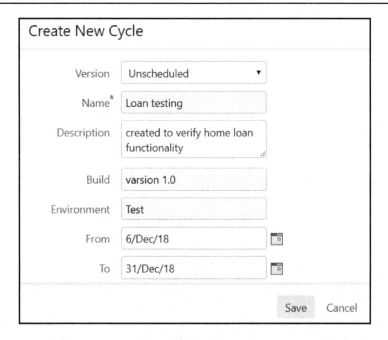

2. As you can see in the following screenshot, once we add a test cycle, it's displayed under the **Cycle Summary** tab. This tab shows us the total number of test cases that have been added under this test cycle, its creator, total executions, start and end dates, and so on:

3. Test cases can be added and removed by clicking on the **+Add Tests** button from the test cycle. We also get the option to select the test cases by their ticket number or by adding them from another test cycle. As you can see in the following screenshot, we have added three test cases using their ticket number:

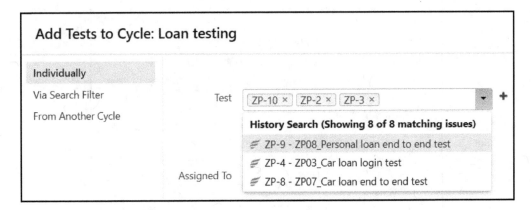

4. In the case of Zephyr, we can update the test status at the test case level or update it at the test step level. The following screenshot shows updating the execution status of the test case at the test case level. By default, Zephyr has the **UNEXECUTED**, **PASS**, **FAIL**, **WIP**, and **BLOCKED** statuses for test execution:

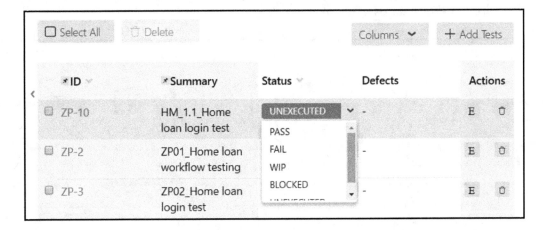

Test Management

Like Zephyr, Test Management tools don't need test plans or test cases to create a test cycle:

1. We can add test cycles by navigating to the **Tests | Cycles** section. Once we click on the **New** button to add a new cycle, we will be shown the following **Details** screen, where we can enter details about this cycle, such as **Folder**, **Status**, **Version**, **Iteration**, **Owner**, **Planned start date** and **Planned end date**, **Description**, and so on:

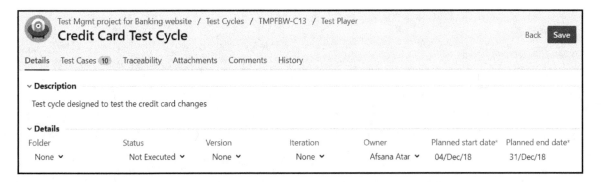

2. Once we have added a new test cycle, we will have access to its unique identifier so that we can differentiate it from other cycles. All of the cycles can be viewed under the **Cycles** tab. In this section, we get the option to **Edit**, start execution, **Delete**, or copy the test cycles:

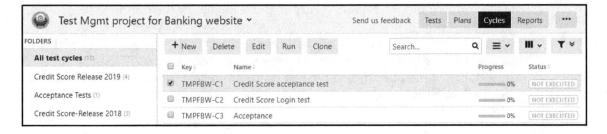

3. We can also add test cases from a selected project to our current test cycle from the **Test Cases** tab. To do this, navigate to the **Test Cases** section and click on the **Add** button, as shown in the following screenshot. We also have the option to view only those test cases that have not been added to the current test cycle. As you can see in the following screenshot, a total of 10 test cases have been selected as part of this test cycle:

4. Once we start the test cycle, the test team can start executing the test cases one by one. During this step-by-step execution, the testers have the option to update the test results at the test step level or at the test case level. As you can see in the following screenshot, once we navigate to the **Test Cycle**, we can see all of the test cases under that cycle. We can start test case execution by clicking on the timer icon. We can also update the test status from **Not Executed** to **In Progress**, **Pass**, **Fail**, or **Blocked**:

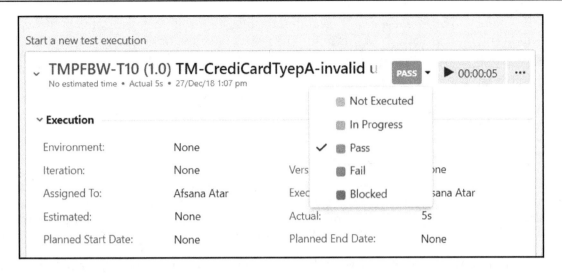

Test execution status

The test execution status defines its current state during the execution phase. The following are the most commonly used test execution statuses:

- **No Run / Not Executed**: A **No Run** or **Not Executed** test status is displayed when the test cases have been added to the test cycles. Its status then gets updated as per the execution results.
- **Passed**: If all the test steps mentioned in the test satisfy the expected results, its status can be marked as **Passed**.
- **Failed**: If any of the test steps fail to meet the expected results, then it can be marked as **Failed**.
- **Not Applicable / Not in scope**: Sometimes, test cases don't need to be executed as part of a current test cycle. In such cases, the test execution status can be updated to **Not Applicable**.
- **Blocked**: If an open defect impacts the testing of one or more test cases, then the relevant test cases can be marked as **Blocked**, with the updated defect number linked to it.

If at any point during the test case's execution the test steps fail, then the status of the entire test case is marked as **Failed**. At this point, the testers have the option to create defects and link them to the test case, either at the step level or at the test case level.

Also, during every test run, testing tools create a new test run instance. Therefore, it is relatively easy to compare the test execution results of a test in the same cycle.

Organizing test cycles

Just like we can prioritize test cases, test cycles can also be ordered based on their priority. Sequentially arranging and reordering test cycles often saves the time and effort of retesting one or more test cases, or even the entire cycle, and helps to verify the most complete or urgent requirements during the initial phase of the test execution cycle.

This helps in the early identification of defects and gives the team enough time to fix and retest any changes. As the execution progresses, the test team updates all of the project stakeholders about the current execution status, which contains information about the total number of test cases being considered for this release, the number of test cases marked as passed, failed, blocked, or no run, along with the number of defects and their current status.

Completing test cycles

Before confirming the closure of test cycles, it is required that you go through the following checklist:

- All of the test cases in that cycle have either been marked as passed or not applicable
- All of the defects related to the test cases have been fixed and retested, and the relevant test cases have been passed
- All of the artifacts that are part of text execution have been generated and attached to the relevant test cases
- All of the artifacts, including the test reports that have been generated, satisfy the exit or test completion criteria as per the test plan
- Test execution reports have been generated and shared with project stakeholders and approved by the relevant approvers

Once this checklist has been gone through and completed, the test team can officially announce the closure of selected test cycles/iterations or execution phases.

Adding test cases to the test cycle from a different project

It's ideal to reuse test cases from previous releases or different projects. We can add them under the current project and use them as part of the current cycle. Let's look at how we can add test cases from different projects to the test cycle.

synapseRT

We can add test cases from another project to test cycles. To do that, click on the **Add Test Case** button in the **Test Case** and search for the desired test cases. As you can see in the following screenshot, we add test cases from another project simply by searching for its ID:

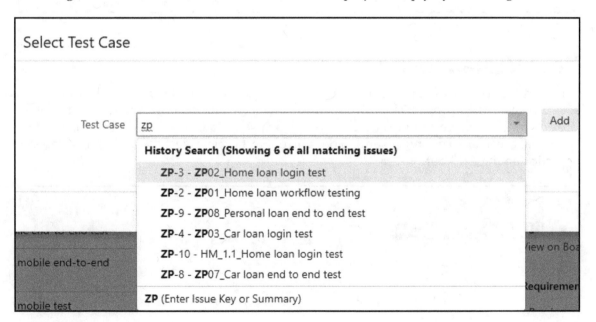

Zephyr

We can add test cases in Zephyr from another project. Navigate to the test cycle and click on the **Add Tests** button; you will see the following screen. Now, search for any test cases from another project by their ticket numbers and add them to the project:

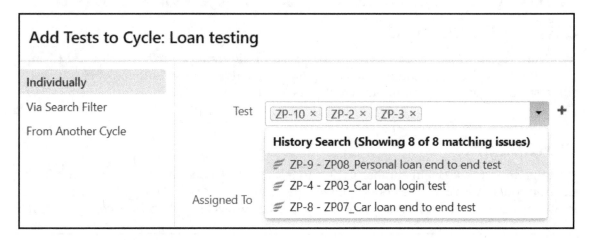

Test Management

While adding test cases to the current test cycle, Test Management gives you the option to select the necessary project. The current project is selected by default. We can select another project from which we want to add test cases. Upon selection, we can see all of the test cases that are available for us to add to our current test cycle. Select the desired test cases and click on the **Add** button:

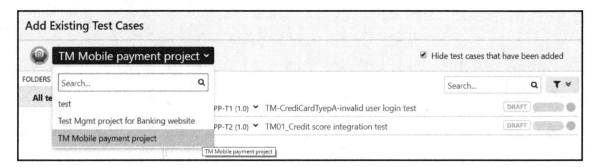

Summary

In this chapter, we learned about the creation and execution of test cycles using Jira plugins. Test cycles in the test execution phase can be created with details such as start and end dates, assigned testers, build numbers, and so on. Test cycles can be modified to add and remove test cases from the current project before starting a test cycle. Test cases can also be reused from previous releases as part of the current release.

In the next chapter, we will discuss the importance of defect management and see how Jira helps us to track and manage defects effectively.

8
Defect Management Phase

Software products can only be trusted if they generate satisfactory results without any faults. Invalid results can have a negative impact on end users. Faulty products can make consumers unhappy and cause frustration. Hence, identifying faults or problems in time can aid developers in delivering a good quality product. However, we need to understand how to classify defects, along with an effective way of reporting them, so as to confirm whether the defect has been resolved.

In this chapter, we will cover the following topics:

- Understanding the importance of logging defects
- Creating new defects
- Linking existing defects to test cases

We will also see how Jira helps us in tracking and managing defects effectively.

Understanding the importance of logging defects

Before understanding the importance of defects, let's understand what a defect actually means in the software industry. When teams start working on a part or component of the project, they start building it with a predefined set of requirements or conditions. Similarly, when the test team creates test cases, they base them on the same set of requirements for the respective components.

Now, during the test execution phase, the test team starts validating the actual product in the test environment by interacting with the application step by step, since the end user will perform the same actions, and compare them with the expected results. If the result matches, testers can pass the selected step or test case. However, if the results are different, then we refer to it as a **defect**.

There are various reasons why the testing team would want to track the issues that occur during the development of the project. Some of the pros and cons are listed here:

- Logging defects in the system helps to track the issues that have been observed during the execution cycle, sprint, and project.
- It helps to identify those requirements that have a large number of defects and require more resources to resolve them. Hence, it helps in organizing resource efforts better.
- It helps to generate artifacts that can be referred to by all the stakeholders of the current project, as well as new resources, as a reference.
- It facilitates collaboration between the team and helps them to focus on the improvement of the application and resolving any issues.
- It makes the application defect-free and gives a better experience to end users.
- Teams can always make reference to the previously logged defects if something has been observed in the recent build or has been reported by the customer.
- It helps the testers or project managers to generate a defect acceptance report (we will be covering this topic in `Chapter 10`, *Test Execution Status Reporting*) and share it with the project stakeholder to make the team aware of existing defects with their current statuses before releasing the product to end users.
- It helps managers to estimate the efforts put forth by the resources to work on a part of the application and, in turn, add the resource billing details and update the project estimation details.

These are a few of the many reasons why teams should invest in comprehensive defect management.

Creating new defects

Simply speaking, deviations from the anticipated results are regarded as defects. There are a few more terms that are used in the industry interchangeably to define a problem, such as a failure, bug, or error. However, any form of issue, no matter what it's called, must be resolved before launching the product.

Software defects can be the result of the following:

- A feature is built based on invalid or incomplete requirements
- A feature is stated in the requirements but the required software for it is missing
- The function used in the code is not returning the expected results, or running in an infinite loop, or accepting an invalid number/type of an input parameter

- Users are not restricted from performing invalid/unauthorized actions
- Error messages as not shown as expected
- Stated and unstated requirements are not met
- Text and images are unreadable
- Invalid code is merged into the build and is deployed in the test environment

Once there is confirmation that the behavior exhibited by the application does not match the stated requirements, which is also confirmed by the development team, then the test team can mark it as a **defect** and log it in the test management system. We will look at how we can create and log defects using Jira plugins in the following sections.

Now that we know what defects are, let's begin with our defect creation process. Test management tools can be used to report newly found defects. It is helpful to trace defects and aids the testers in collaborating with the team smoothly. Before creating new defects, it is essential to check whether a similar defect already exists in the system and what its current status is. Defects can only be reported and fixed successfully if they are reproducible; hence, it is necessary to reproduce it a few times before logging it in the system.

It is recommended that the following checklist be observed before logging any defects. Though this is a common checklist, more steps can be added as per your requirements:

- An application's behavior specified in the requirements document is different from the results achieved
- Verify that testing is being performed in the correct environment with the expected configuration
- Check that the application's build version is correct and that it has been configured as per testing requirements
- Check that all the required services of the application are up and running
- Check that the application is compatible with the specified operating system, browser, or third-party application
- Check that the test is being performed from the specified state of an application with valid test data
- Check that the user role has all the necessary permissions to perform the actions as mentioned in the test case
- Check that there is connectivity between the application, server, and databases

Adding more details to the defect helps developers identify an initial location in the specific part of the code to start debugging while performing root cause analysis, instead of checking the entire product or module. Let's see what details should be added while logging the defects.

For more information about defect management, please check the article on defect management that is available at `https://www.red-gate.com/simple-talk/dotnet/software-delivery/a-primer-on-defect-managment/`.

How to create defects using Jira plugins

Generally, test management tools provide a template with some of the default fields to log the defects. However, we can always be more descriptive, for example, by specifying the following:

- A unique identifier to identify the defect
- A summary of the defect
- Actions to be performed to reproduce the defect
- Variations between the actual and expected results
- The test environment used to perform the test
- Preconditions, such as the state of the application under test
- The version of the application under test with the configuration details
- The build version of the code deployed in the test environment
- The test data used to perform the test
- The defect creation date
- The current status of the defect
- The name of the assignee who will be working on the defect
- The name of the reporter who is logging the defect
- The priority and severity of the defect to determine the impact of the defect on the application and the urgency in terms of fixing it
- The project/sprint/module name where it occurred
- Requirement details concerning when it is not working as expected
- The related test case/test step that has been marked as failed
- Artifacts, such as screenshots, log files, error descriptions, and the test data used to execute the test case, the output results generated, if any, and so on

Since we now know the template, let's create defects using the Jira plugins.

Designing and managing defect workflows in Jira

Defect workflow can be customized to have its own set of statuses that a defect issue type can undergo. Organizations can have their own set of workflows. Let's look at some of the recommended statuses that a defect should go through. This is also referred to as a defect life cycle:

- **DRAFT**: A defect can be set on **DRAFT** when the tester still needs to provide more details in relation to it
- **NEW/OPEN**: This status can be set for the defect when all the details are added and it is ready to be assigned to a developer
- **ASSIGNED**: Once the project team identifies a developer who will be working on the logged defect, the status of the defect can be set to **ASSIGNED** and should be assigned to the developer in question
- **IN PROGRESS**: Once a defect gets assigned, the developer can change the status of the defect to **IN PROGRESS** to indicate that the developer is working to fix the issue
- **FIXED**: The developer can change the defect status to **FIXED** once the required code changes are implemented and it is made available for the testers to verify the changes
- **NOT FIXED**: The tester sets the defect status as **NOT FIXED** if the defect is still reproducible and the fix is not satisfactory as per the requirements
- **CLOSED**: If the fixed defect is working as expected and it matches the stated requirements, then the tester closes the defect and sets its status as **CLOSED**
- **REOPEN**: If a previously resolved defect is now reoccurring, then the tester can change the status of the defect to **REOPEN**
- **NOT APPLICABLE**: If the newly created defect is not related to the verified changes, then the developer can change the status of the defect to **NOT APPLICABLE**
- **NOT A DEFECT**: If the application or feature is behaving as expected, then the developer can change the status of the defect to **NOT A DEFECT**
- **NOT REPRODUCIBLE**: If the developer is unable to recreate the defect in the same environment and build version, then its status can be updated to **NOT REPRODUCIBLE**
- **DUPLICATE**: If a similar defect already exists in the system, then the development team can update the defect status to **DUPLICATE**
- **VERIFIED**: If the code changes for the defect have been verified by the tester, then its status can be marked as **VERIFIED**

- **PENDING**: If the defect verification is on hold due to the unavailability of the environment, test data, or resources, then its status can be updated to **PENDING**
- **DEFERRED**: The defect status can be marked as **DEFERRED** if the team decides to work on the fix in the upcoming sprints or release

Since we are familiar with the defect workflow now, let's create one using Jira:

1. In order to create a customized workflow in Jira, we need to add a workflow scheme and add a customized workflow to this scheme. The option to add a workflow scheme is available under **Admin | Issues | Workflows | Workflow Scheme**. Assign a name to this defect workflow scheme, such as `DefectWorkflowScheme-1`, add a **Description**, and then click on the **Add** button to create a scheme:

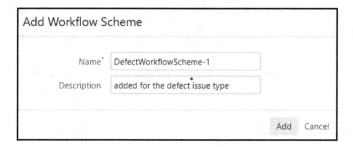

2. As shown in the following screenshot, the customized defect workflow has various statuses similar to the ones we discussed earlier. This workflow has been categorized as **defect workflow**, which will be added to a workflow scheme:

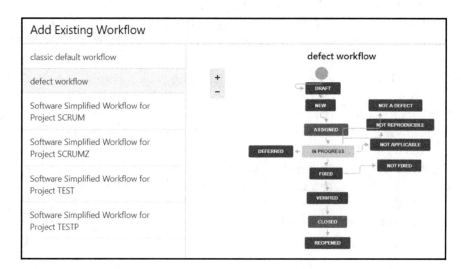

3. After selecting the existing workflow, click on the **Next** button. The following screenshot shows issue types that you want to apply to this workflow. Select the **Defect** issue type and click on the **Finish** button, as shown:

4. Once you add a defect workflow, it can be viewed from the **Project settings | Issues | Workflows** section. As shown in the following screenshot, the current project has two types of workflow, namely the **Jira Workflow** and the **defect workflow**. The **defect workflow** field has an associated issue type as a **defect**. Here, it will prompt you to publish the changes and as soon as you publish, the newly added workflow will be added to the defect issue type:

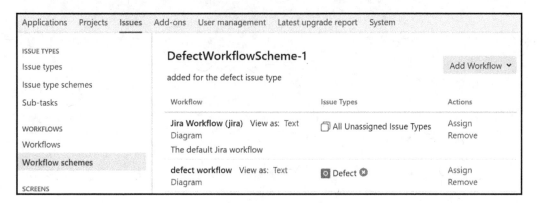

5. Now, navigate to the **Project | Project Settings | Issues** sections. Here, you need to customize your project to have a **Defect** issue type. As shown in the following screenshot, we have added a **Defect** issue type to the **Issue Types for Current Scheme** section so that it will be added to your current project scheme:

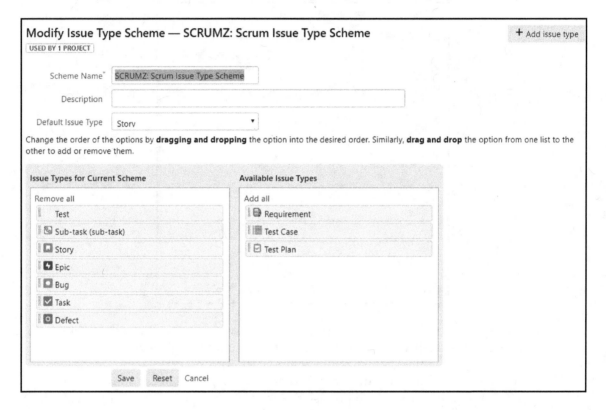

6. Click **Save** and our defect workflow is created.

synapseRT

synapseRT has additional issue types, including requirement, test case, and test plan, but it has a missing defect issue type. From the previous section, we now know how to add defect issue types with the customized workflows to our project. After adding the issue type, follow these steps to log a defect:

1. Since a defect is another issue type, click on the **Create** button to create a defect, select the project in question, and then select the issue type as **Defect**, as shown in the following screenshot. Then, click on the **Next** button:

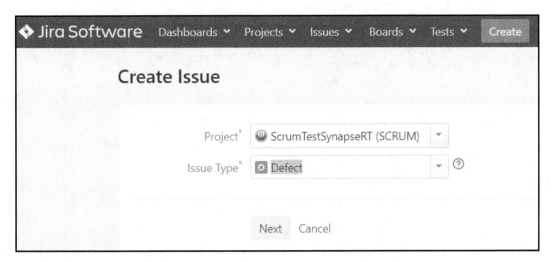

2. This will load the issue description page with the header **Create Issue**, as shown in the following screenshot. On this page, provide the details, including the **Summary**, the **Reporter**, the **Description** which includes steps taken to reproduce the defect—the actual and expected behavior, the preconditions, test data, the **Priority**, **Assignee** details, and **Linked Issues**. After entering all the necessary details required, click on the **Create** button to create a defect:

Create Issue

Project	**ScrumTestSynapseRT**
Issue Type	**O Defect**
Summary*	Exception thrown after clicking on login button
Reporter*	atar.afsana@consulseer.in
	Start typing to get a list of possible matches.
Component/s	**None**
Description	Style∨ **B** *I* U A ∨ A° ∨ &∨ ⋮☰ ⋮☰ ☺∨ +∨ ⌃

Steps to Reproduce Defect:

1. Launch the application
2. Enter valid username and password
3. Click on Login

Actual: It throws an exception on the screen with error 404-page not found

Expected: Homepage should be loaded

Visual   Text

Fix Version/s	**None**
Priority	↑ Highest ⊘
Labels	
	Begin typing to find and create labels or press down to select a suggested label.
Linked Issues	blocks
Issue	+
	Begin typing to search for issues to link. If you leave it blank, no link will be made.
Assignee	atar.afsana@consulseer.in Assign to me
Epic Link	
	Choose an epic to assign this issue to.
Sprint	
	Jira Software sprint field

Create   Cancel

3. Once you create the defect, Jira will automatically generate the unique ticket number to identify this issue type. Defect goes through different stages as per the designed workflow, which we will see in the next section. As shown in the following screenshot, Jira has added a unique ID as **SCRUM-7** for the defect. The current status of the defect is **ASSIGNED** and the next status as per the customized workflow is **under development**. It also shows the nature of this issue type as **Defect**, and its **Priority**, as set by the reporter, is **Medium**:

We can add the defect issue type to Zephyr and to the Test Management project as well. Since it is a new issue type, the steps for creating a defect in Zephyr and Test Management remain the same.

Linking existing defects to test cases

Establishing a relationship between defects and test cases helps to identify the impact of a defect on the current execution of test cases. If a single defect impacts more than one test case, then the testers can link the same defect to all the impacted test cases and update the test case status as **Blocked**.

However, apart from the impact analysis, it also helps in generating the traceability matrix where the requirements are linked to the test cases and test cases are linked to the defect. Defects can be linked to the test case at the test case level or test step level. If a test case has a greater number of test steps, and there are multiple defects observed for the same test cases, then in such cases, it makes more sense to link these defects at the test step level to identify at which step specifically the error has occurred.

Changing a test case status with regard to defects

Whenever the test team logs a defect and links it to the relevant test case, the status of the test case is updated as **Failed**. Now, the test case status remains as **failed**, unless and until the related defect is either closed or deferred. Once the defect is closed, the relevant test case status is updated to **Passed**.

However, if the defect is linked at the test step level, the steps that worked as expected are updated as **Passed**. The step where a defect has been observed is updated as **Failed** and the remaining steps that the tester is not able to execute remain in the default **Not executed** or **Not run** status.

Let's link the defect to the test cases using the Jira plugins.

synapseRT

synapseRT gives an option to link a defect either at the test case level or test step level. Select any test case in synapseRT and create an ad hoc run. During the execution, it creates a new test run and shows the options to either link the existing defect or create new ones under the **Run Attributes** section. We also have an option to update the test status at the test step level.

In the following screenshot, step one has been marked as failed and it has an associated **SCRUM-7** defect at the test step level. However, there are two defects, **SCRUM-7** and SCRUM-5, linked to the test case level. Since one test step has failed here, the status of the entire test case gets updated as **FAILED**:

If multiple test cases are blocked due to a single defect during the test cycle, then the same defect can be linked to the test cases and their status can be updated as **BLOCKED**. The following screenshot depicts this behavior:

There are three test cases in total. One has failed because of the defect, and the same defect is blocking the remaining two test cases in the current test cycle.

Zephyr

In the case of Zephyr, once we start executing the test case from the selected test cycle, we can update the test status at the test case level or test step level.

While executing the test, we also have an option to link a defect at the test step level or at the test case level. As shown in the following screenshot, since one step has been marked as **FAIL**, the status of the entire test case has changed to **FAIL**. The following steps are marked as **BLOCKED**. In the **Defect** section, it has a defect linked to it as SCRUMZ-3:

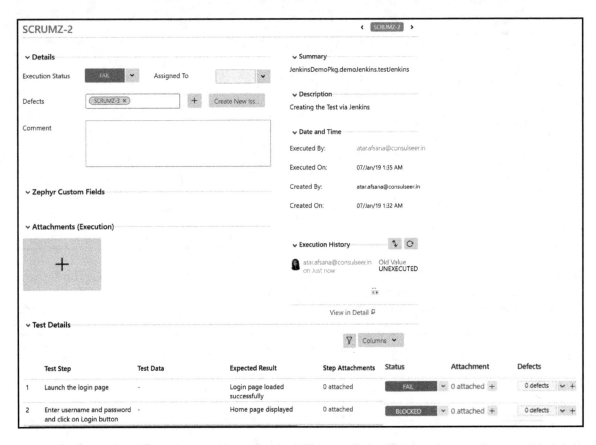

After completing this run, the status of the test execution and its linked defects can be viewed at the test cycle level. In the following screenshot, we can see an Ad hoc test cycle has a test case named SCRUMZ-2, which is linked to the defect, SCRUMZ-3:

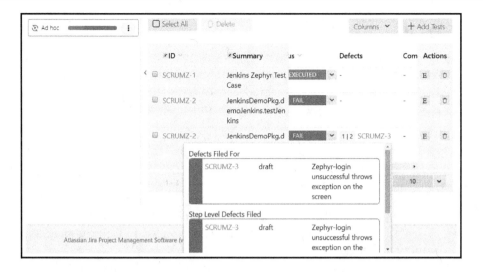

Test Management

The Test Management tool also has an option to link a defect and update the status of the test step at the test step and test case levels.

As shown in the following screenshot, the test case `TESTP-T2` is marked as having failed at step 1 and its **ISSUES** section indicates the linked defects. In our case, this is `TESTP-1`. The remaining steps are marked as **BLOCKED**:

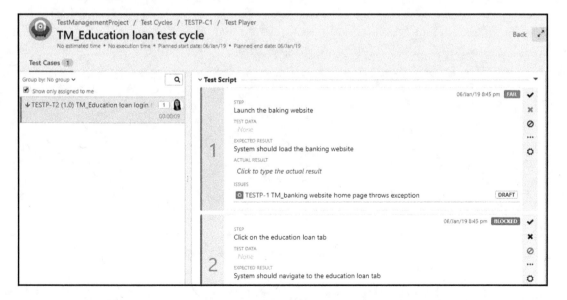

Summary

In this chapter, we learned about the defect creation and management process. We learned to identify defects and understand their possible root causes. We also looked at the preliminary checks that should be performed before reporting defects, as well as the details that should be provided while logging the defects in the system.

We then learned to create defects in Jira by having a customized issue type, such as **defect**, and a customized workflow. In order to create traceability, we learned how to link defects to the relevant test cases with the help of Jira plugins, either at the test step or the test case level during the test execution phase.

In the next chapter, we will discuss how Jira issues can be used to track project requirements. We will also see ways in which Jira can be used to link requirements to test cases as requirement coverage.

Section 5: Test Management - Monitor and Control

5

We will learn how Jira can help you to define a strategy for monitoring and controlling projects using different types of reports.

This section will include the following chapters:

- Chapter 9, *Requirement Management*
- Chapter 10, *Test Execution Status Reporting*

Requirement Management 9

Requirements are customer needs that are defined in relation to a project. They are tracked using the requirement number or ticket number in Jira to monitor and control the project's progress. Linking requirements to the test cases helps the project team to estimate not only the effort required in terms of resources and the time required to validate the linked requirement, but also helps to understand which requirement has more defects during the execution phase.

In this chapter, we will be covering the following topics:

- Creating the Jira issue type as a requirement
- Establishing relations between requirements and test cases

We will also look at how Jira helps us to define the project requirements using the Jira issue types.

Creating the Jira issue type as requirement

In Jira, we have default issue types, such as Epic, Story, Task, Sub-task, and Bug. These issue types give us flexibility to define our own issue types as per the project's requirements. However, each of these issue types can be treated as a requirement. Once the requirements are defined and logged in the system, it becomes easy to track and manage them. We learned how to define requirements in Chapter 3, *Understanding Components of Testing with Jira*. So now, let's create them in Jira.

Creating requirements

Jira has a predefined set of fields to create Jira tickets. Additionally, we can add customized fields as required according to the selected issue type. Any requirement issue type should generally contain the following:

- The purpose of the requirement or the task that the team is expected to accomplish
- The detailed description that breaks the complex requirement down into further details and specifications
- The issue type's priority
- The issue type's current status

The following details are added while creating a requirement issue type:

Requirement field	Description
Requirement ID	This field helps to identify requirements uniquely. Most of the time, business requirements are prepared by business analysts and labeled with the IDs as required.
Summary	This field provides a short description of the requirement in terms of the goal or target that is expected to be accomplished.
Detailed description	This field defines the goal of the requirement in detail. If it has various components or modules that need to be worked on, or any other technical specification, then all such items can be specified in this field.
Priority	This field defines the urgency in terms of working on the requirement and releasing it for use to end users.
Status	The status of the requirements helps project stakeholders know the current status and progress of the selected requirement.
Date of creation	Generally, requirement management tools add a time and date for the requirements when they get created in the system.
Approvers	Often, requirements must go through the approval phase. Once agreed and approved by the project stakeholders in question, the developers assigned to this task can start working on them. This field can be used to list the required approvers for the specified requirement.
Approved date	Once requirements have been approved by the person concerned, the system automatically updates the approver's details, as well as the time and date when they were approved.

Assignee	This field decides the next responsible person who needs to take an action in relation to the requirement. This may be a business analyst, approver, developer, or tester.
Reporter	This field automatically gets added by the system with the name of the person in question who logged the requirement in the system.
Build number	Once the requirements are converted in the form of code, reviewed, and are ready to deploy for testing, they can be linked to a build number. The build number helps testers, as well as developers, to debug and analyze code easily and pinpoint which requirement is failing.
Application version	If the application is built in a different version, and has a different set of requirements, adding an application version while creating the requirements can help the project team to differentiate and manage requirements effectively.
Release number	If the project has various releases, then it's a good option to link requirements to the related release. It not only helps in managing the requirements, but also helps in generating the release specific reports and tracking their progress.
Project name	Requirements are usually project-specific. Hence, it's a good idea to add project details while creating the requirement.
Linked test cases	Linking test cases to requirements helps in understanding the test coverage. Also, it helps in generating the traceability matrix. Hence, once the test team is ready with the test cases, these can be linked to the specified requirement.
Comments	If there is any additional information, this can be added to the comments field.
Dependency	If there are any dependent requirements, or if there is any dependency in terms of tools, another module, resource, or approvals, all such things should be defined in this field.

Organizations often customize them for specifying the requirements. Hence, you might observe variations of this format.

Prioritizing requirements

Requirement prioritization is done based on the need and urgency to deliver the feature to the end users. While prioritizing the requirements, the project team also considers its complexity and the efforts required to accomplish the requested tasks. The project team can take actions based on the level of priority.

For example, if the feature request is of critical priority, that means that its importance is very high and its timeline very short. Hence, all the things needed to achieve the aforementioned tasks, such as data, tools, permissions, a skill set, and resources, are acquired within a short period and the project team tries to achieve its goal as per the set timelines.

Jira has four different priority types assigned to any issue type by default:

- **Critical**: These are the requirements that are very urgent and that have a high impact on the business. These aspects need to be addressed and, fixed in the shortest time so that they are delivered to end users on an urgent basis.
- **High**: These are the requirements that need to be addressed and worked on as soon as possible. However, the timeline is generally specified by the project stakeholders.
- **Medium**: These are medium priority requirements that are worked on after all the critical or high priority items are delivered, since their urgency level is medium.
- **Low**: Low priority requirements have minimal urgency. Hence, they are the last items in the developer's priority list to be worked on. Sometimes, tasks/subtasks with a low priority status can also be moved to another release or sprint if the project team needs more time to focus on the most critical/high-priority items in the current release/sprint.

Requirement status

The requirement status helps the project team to know its current state as well as giving it direction to be ready for the next course of action. Setting the status is part of the workflow. Hence, organizations may have a customized status that can vary by project or even by issue type.

In general, the following statuses are useful for requirement issue types:

- **Draft**: As the name suggests, this status can be used if there are further details that need to be added by the members responsible. Generally, a business analyst is responsible for creating the business requirements. If not, then the project leader creates them in the system.
- **Draft complete**: Once all the requirement details are added, their status can be updated as **Draft complete**.
- **Assigned for approval**: If the requirement needs approval, this can be assigned to the person concerned and its status can be updated as **Assigned for approval**.

- **Pending approval**: As the name suggests, if approval is pending for any reason, the requirement status can be updated as **Pending approval**.
- **Approved**: Once the requirements are reviewed by the approvals and it looks good to begin development, their status can be marked as **Approved**.
- **Selected for development**: Requirements in the **Approved** status that have been added to the current sprint or release for development are updated as having a **Selected for development** status.
- **In progress**: When developers are working on converting the requirements into code, their status can be updated as **In progress**.
- **Ready for review**: Once the code changes are implemented in the system, developers can update their status as **Ready for review** and assign them to the development team for peer review.
- **Review completed**: If there are any comments during the peer review process, the developer in question works on them and makes the code changes. After updating the code as per the comments, its status is updated as **Review completed**.
- **Ready to test**: Developers make the code ready to deploy in the test environment by adding it to the required code branch. It is then assigned to the test team by updating the status as *Ready to test*.
- **Testing in progress**: Once the project team identifies the tester who will be working on verifying the selected requirements, they get assigned to that tester and the ticket status is updated as **Testing in progress**.
- **Testing completed**: Testers design test cases and start validation against the specified requirement in the test execution phase. Once all the test cases linked to the specific requirements are either marked as **Passed** or **N/A**, the status of the requirement can be updated as **Testing completed**.
- **Ready to release**: All the verified requirements for which testing has been performed, along with all the bugs that have been fixed and retested, and that are ready to deploy in production, can be marked as **Ready to release**.
- **Released**: After deploying the selected requirement in the production environment for end users to use, its status is updated as **Released**.
- **Closed**: Once the requirements are deployed successfully in the production environment, and provided there are no other newly created dependent requirements or issues that need to be developed, their status can be marked as **Closed**.

Managing requirement artifacts

Requirements can be created in various formats, while different types of artifacts are possible, including the following:

- **Project charter**: This initiates the project.
- **Project's approved requirement document**: It contains the approved requirements at high-level.
- **Project's high-level and low-level design documents**: These define the project architecture in detail.
- **Project plan**: This includes details regarding the scope, time, cost, budget, and other relevant plans, including a change management strategy plan, and a resource allocation plan. It also defines the list of acceptable deliverables at the end of each phase and their formats.
- **Project's related third-party tool documents**: These are going to be used in relation to the current project, such as product information, tutorials, or user permissions that are required to access the tools.
- **Risk mitigation strategy and action plan**: This is used to understand the project risks and the steps required to mitigate them.
- **Knowledge base repository**: This contains all the documents released in relation to the current project, as well as any other relevant projects that can be used by the project team. Examples include lessons learned and retrospective documents from previous releases that can be referenced by the project team.
- **Training documents**: These are the resource training-related documents and videos, if any.
- **Roles and responsibilities**: These are the documents relating to resource roles and responsibilities.
- **Project meetings**: This includes project planning, weekly and/or daily meetings or calls, discussion reports, including minutes of meetings or any emails that have been used to confirm the requirements or conditions for the project features.
- **Project progress report**: This report is generated at the end of each sprint or every phase of product development. Examples include sprint reports, epic reports, project burndown charts, test execution reports, test cycle reports, and test plan reports.

Since there are various types of documents generated before, during, and at the end of the project, managing the project repository as per the sprint or release is necessary.

Establishing relations between requirements and test cases

The first step in setting up the traceability matrix is to link the test cases that were designed based on the requirements with the relevant requirements documented in the system. The traceability matrix helps the test team to understand the test coverage and manage test cases appropriately by adding or removing test cases as applicable.

During the test execution phase, this link helps the test team to understand which requirements are failing or taking more time to execute. Test managers can then decide on a strategy to overcome these issues and allocate more resources or time as needed.

Let's see how the test cases can be linked to the requirements using Jira plugins.

synapseRT

To link test cases to different issue types in Jira, we need to configure the issue types as **Requirements** from the **Configuration** section. Once configured properly, those issue types will have a test case section that can be used to link the test cases to the tickets. Now, let's observe the following steps to link the test case:

1. As shown in the following screenshot, a Story issue type has been configured as a requirement. Hence, it has a **Test Cases** section that enables users to either create a new test case or link an existing test case to the story. The following screenshot has a test case, SCRUM-11, which is linked to the story SCRUM-14:

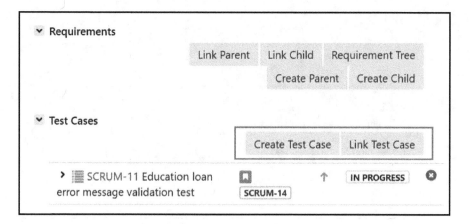

2. The **Create Test Case** option will open a **Create** issue page where you can create a new test case and it will link to the story automatically. In order to link the existing test case, click on the **Link Test Case** button and, as shown in the following screenshot, it gives you the option to **Select Test Case** and link it to the ticket:

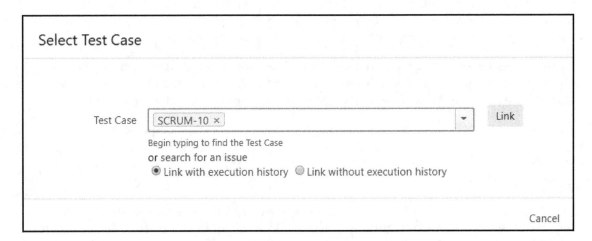

3. Since the test case issued in synapseRT is another issue type, we also have the option to link a requirement from a test case issue type. In order to do so, open the test case issue and click on the **Link** button from the **Select Requirement** section. As demonstrated in the following screenshot, select the requirement by its ID and click on **Link**:

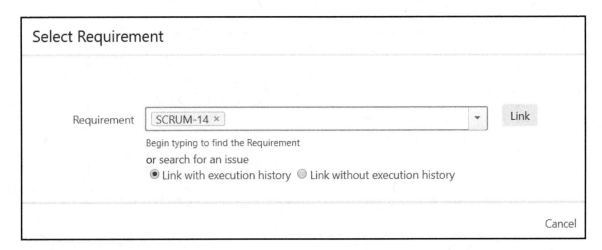

4. After linking the requirement, if you now go back to the **Requirement** section of the test case, you will see that Jira has created a link between the test case and a story from the test case issue type. As shown in the following screenshot, along with the **Requirement** section, we can also add details regarding the **Test Suite** the test case belongs to, as well as the **Test Plan**:

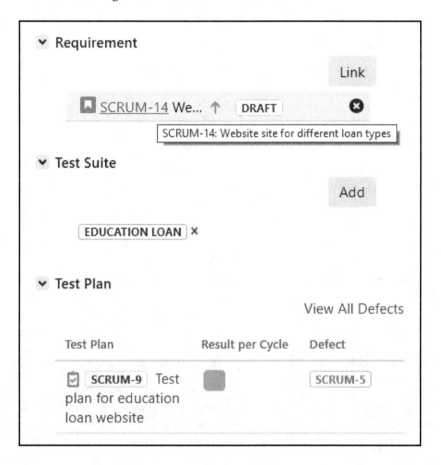

5. We also have an option in synapseRT, called **Test Plan** issue type, to view the test case coverage for the selected requirement. In order to view the coverage first, we need to add the same set of test cases to the requirement issue type, as well as in the test plan. After that, if you open the test plan issue, you can view the test case coverage from the **Requirement** section, as shown in the following screenshot. In this case, the requirement coverage is **100.0%**, since all test cases planned to the requirement are linked to the requirement issue type, as well as added in the test plan to verify the functionality:

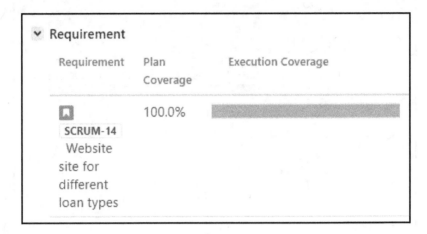

Zephyr

In Zephyr, we can establish the relationship between the requirement issue type and test cases by linking the issues.

1. In order to do this, first create a requirement issue type in Zephyr. On the **Create issue** screen, there is a field called **Linked Issues**. Click on it. This reveals the following screenshot, from where related issues—in our case, a test case—can be linked:

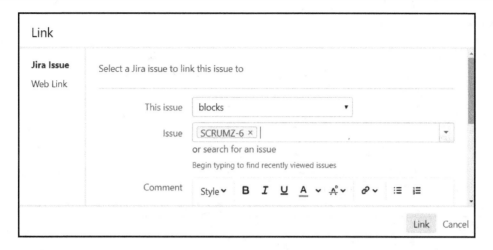

2. Once we are done linking all the test cases to the requirement issue type, the links can be viewed from the **Issue Links** section. Now, since the test case in Zephyr is also an issue type, by following the same steps, we can link requirements to the test case issue. As shown in the following screenshot, the test case issue type SCRUMZ-5 has linked to its related requirement story issue type, SCRUMZ-6, and this is added under the **Issue Links** section of the test case:

Test Management

In the case of Test Management for the Jira plugin, we can add test cases to the requirement issue type from the **Traceability** section. This section provides multiple options to either create or link test cases, or even test cycles:

1. Click on the + icon from the **Traceability** section of the **Story** issue type.
2. Select an option, **Add Existing Test Case**. This shows the following screen for selecting the existing test cases. It shows all the existing test cases in the **Add Existing Test Cases** window. Select the checkbox for the desired test cases, and click on the **Add** button to add these test cases to the requirement issue type:

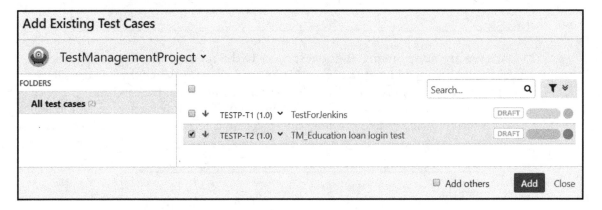

3. After linking the existing test cases to the story type, all the linked test cases can be viewed from the **Traceability** section. As shown in the following screenshot, in the case of the story TESTP-2, we have linked two test cases, TESTP-T2(1.0) and TESTP-T3(1.0):

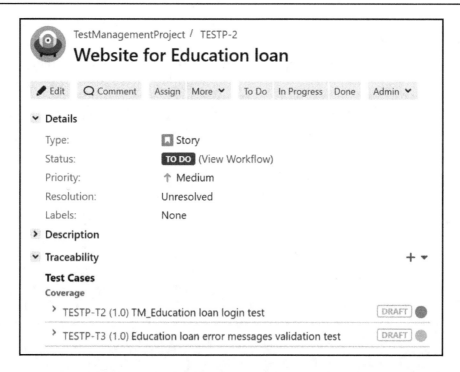

4. We can also link requirements from the test cases. In order to do so, navigate to the **Tests** section, open any existing test, and click on the **Traceability** tab. Click on the **Add** button in the **Issues** section and select the desired issues that you want to link to the test case. An issue can be searched from within the current or another project. Click on the checkbox for the desired issue that you want to link and then click on the **Add** button.

5. After adding the requirement, it should be displayed under the **Traceability | Issues** section. As shown in the following screenshot, we have linked the TESTP-T2 test case with the TESTP-2 requirement from the **Test Case Traceability** section:

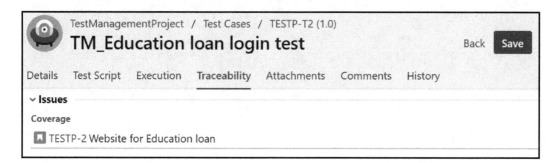

Summary

In this chapter, we learned how we can effectively manage and document requirements in Jira. We saw how Jira issues can be utilized to track requirements for the testing phase. We then understood how test coverage can be traced using the traceability matrix. Furthermore, we created the traceability matrix using each of the Jira plugins by linking requirements to the relevant test cases.

In the next chapter, we will explore how Jira can help monitor and control projects using reports, and we will detail the various reports offered by Jira.

10
Test Execution Status Reporting

Project status reports give us insights into a project's health throughout the project development phase. This helps in monitoring and controlling project progress so that deliveries meet the required quality standards and deadlines. There are various types of reports available through Jira. The main goal of reports is to identify any runtime issues and obstacles or last-minute changes that need to be implemented. Reports help all project stakeholders to be on the same page about the current status of the project and allow them to make democratic decisions on containing any deviations from the plan.

Project managers plan ahead in order to identify risks and create risk mitigation strategies as well. They also address activities in change management and communication management. Reporting is a part of communication management.

In this chapter, we will be covering the following topics:

- Test plan execution reports
- Ad hoc test run reports
- Requirement-based reports
- Defect matrix reports
- Test suite reports
- Burndown charts

We will also cover reports created during the test execution phase of the project, as Jira plugins are useful for generating these reports.

Test plan execution reports

During the test execution phase, test execution is carried out in terms of test cycles, or iterations. Each iteration or test cycle has a set of planned test cases. It is useful to track the progress of test execution based on the cycle or iteration. If the iteration or test cycle is a part of the test plan, then generating a test plan execution report gives us clarity about the currently executed test cases and their statuses.

Let's generate a test plan execution report using Jira plugins.

synapseRT

synapseRT has an option to generate a test plan execution report, with the help of which a project team can track the progress of the current execution:

1. synapseRT has a **SynapseRT Reports** tab from where we can select the **Test Plan Execution Report** option to customize and generate the test plan execution report.
2. As shown in the following screenshot, we have the option to select the **Test Plan** and specific cycle, or all the cycles, along with the test case execution status. After selecting all the appropriate values, click on the **Generate Report** button to create the report:

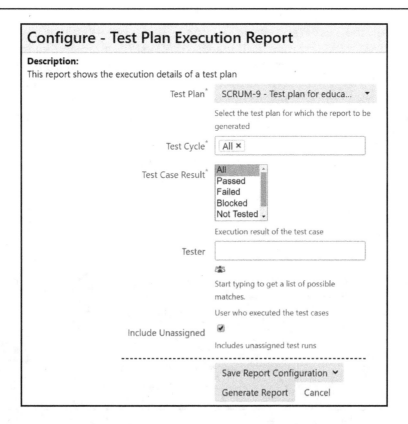

3. This creates the report shown in the following screenshot. The report lists all the test cases that belong to the selected test cycle, their current statuses in the **Result** column, the **Tester** to whom the test case has been assigned, and who has executed the test case (in the **Tested By** column). There are a few more details, such as **Executed On** (which specifies the date and time of execution), **Defects**, **Estimate**, and **Effort**. We also have an option to extract this report in Excel format:

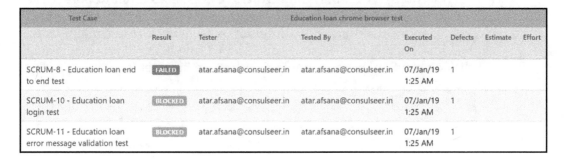

4. Through the **Test Plan** section, we can also view the status of the current execution of the test plan. Navigate to the **Test Plan** tab and go to the **Unresolved Plans** section. It lists all the test plans that do not have a closed status. Simply click on the drop-down icon and it shows the execution progress segregated by test cycles. As shown in the following screenshot, we have two test cycles with the status as **ACTIVE**. It also shows details such as **Test Run**, **Defect**, and their current **Status**:

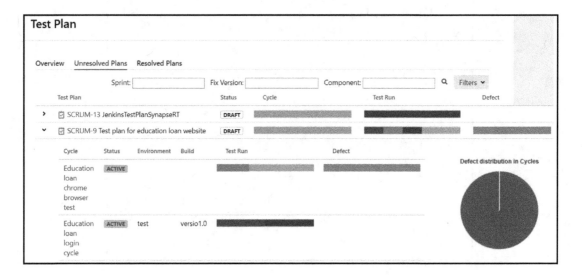

Zephyr

In Zephyr, we can generate a test case execution report to view the progress of each cycle and its associated test cases:

1. In order to generate the report, navigate to the **Report** section in Jira. There are two main sections—**All reports** and **Other**. **Testcase Execution Report** is listed under the **Other** section. Click on it to create one. As shown in the following screenshot, doing this shows the configuration page for customizing the report as per the project, test cycles, versions, and so on. Provide the appropriate values and click on **Next**. In the following screenshot, we have set the number of test cycles as 3:

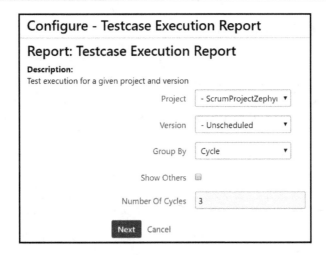

2. The following report is then generated. It lists the number of test cases on the y axis and groups them together by cycle on the x axis. For example, the `Loan testing` test cycle has total of six test cases, of which two have a passed status and are hence colored in green, two are in red (failed), one is blocked, and one did not execute:

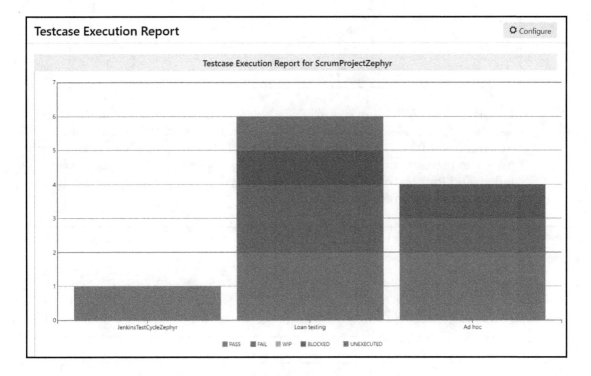

Test Management

Test Management has an option to create a test plan consisting of test cycles:

1. In order to generate a test report by test plan, navigate to the **Tests** tab and go to the **Reports** section. This shows a number of options for generating the report; select the **Test execution results by test plan** option. It lets you customize the report as per the project, start and end date, and execution based on the most recent or all. After selecting all the required options, click on the **Generate** button:

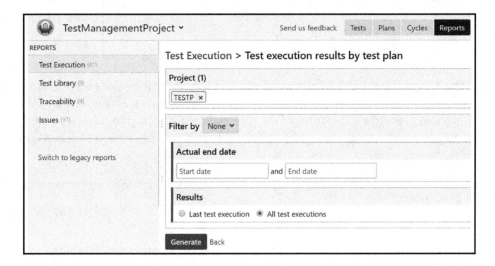

2. It generates the following report. The y axis indicates the number of test plans selected and the x axis shows the number of test cases with their current execution statuses. The following screenshot shows that we have a total of eight test cases planned, out of which one had been blocked, one has passed, two have failed, and four test cases were not executed. We also have an option to either print or export the report in Excel format:

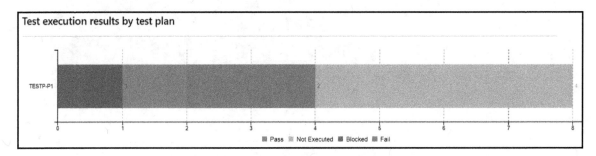

Ad hoc test run reports

Ad hoc test run reports indicate the number of times a selected test case has been executed as a part of an ad hoc test run. In this case, the test case is not a part of any test plan and is executed independently. It's also useful to track its status changes. If any artifacts are attached during the ad hoc test run, such as test data, screenshots, or logs, testers can use this information to compare the results from its last execution. Jira plugins have the option to generate such reports. Let's create them one by one.

synapseRT

synapseRT has the option to view the ad hoc test run details at an individual test case level from the **Ad hoc Test Run** section. As shown in the following screenshot, the selected test case has been executed three times and its status varies from **BLOCKED** to **FAILED** and **PASSED**. It also shows details such as the ID of the test run, who it was executed by, the execution date and time, and relevant defects, if any:

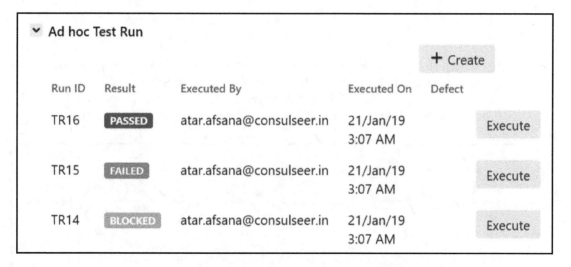

Ad hoc test run reports can be generated for all test cases:

1. In order to generate such reports, navigate to the **SynapseRT Reports** tab and select the option as **Ad hoc Test Run Report**. As shown in the following screenshot, enter the required details, such as **Execution type** and **Start Date** and **End Dates**, and click on the **Generate Report** button:

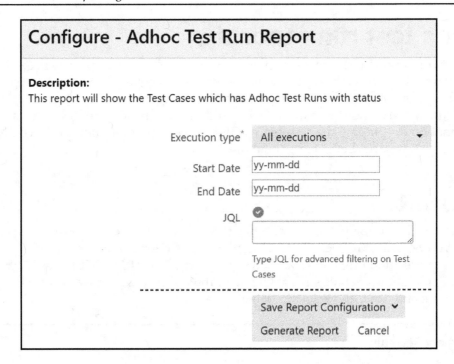

2. As shown in the following screenshot, the ad hoc test run report gets generated. It shows details such as the names of the test cases; their current status in the **Result** column; who tested it, in the **Tested By** column; the execution date and time in **Executed on**; and linked defects, if any, in the **Defects** column:

Test Cases	Result	Tested By	Executed on	Estimate	Effort	Defects
SCRUM-16 test to verify forgot password functionality	PASSED	atar.afsana@consulseer.in	21/Jan/19 3:07 AM			0
SCRUM-16 test to verify forgot password functionality	FAILED	atar.afsana@consulseer.in	21/Jan/19 3:07 AM			0
SCRUM-16 test to verify forgot password functionality	BLOCKED	atar.afsana@consulseer.in	21/Jan/19 3:07 AM			0
SCRUM-8 Education loan end to end test	FAILED	atar.afsana@consulseer.in	07/Jan/19 1:14 AM			2

Zephyr

Zephyr has an ad hoc test cycle to which test cases can be added and executed. We can view the status of the selected cycle from the **Cycle Summary** tab:

1. Navigate to the **Tests | Test Summary | Cycle Summary** tab. It shows all the test cycles for all the releases.
2. Hover a mouse on the ad hoc cycle and observe that it lists the current status of all the test cases in this cycle. It also indicates a color bar to show the progress of the status in green, red, and blue to indicate statuses as pass, fail, and blocked. As shown in the following screenshot, the ad hoc test cycle has a total of four test cases, out of which two, which is **50%** of total test cases, are in the **PASS** status, while one has its status as **FAIL**, and one is in the **BLOCKED** status:

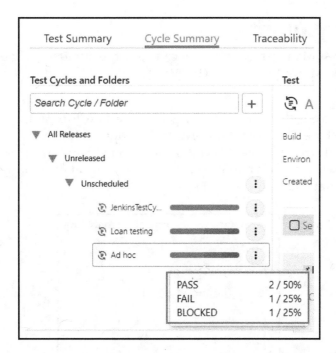

3. It also gives an option to view the status of individual test cases from **Test Case | Test Executions**. The following screenshot shows that the selected test case has been executed three times, out of which two executions were part of the ad hoc execution and one execution was part of the test cycle's Loan testing. It also shows the execution status each time it has been executed, and so on:

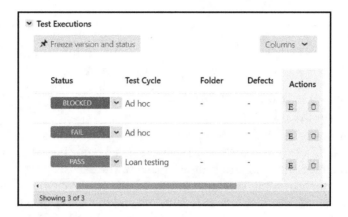

Test Management

In the case of the Test Management tool, we can view the number of times a selected test case has been executed by navigating to the **Reports | Test Execution | Test execution results (list)** report:

1. In order to create this report, navigate to the **Test | Reports | Test Execution** tab and select the **Test execution results (list)** option. Enter the required details, such as the cycle that you want to test. As shown in the following screenshot, we have selected the test cycle and project. After entering all the required details, click on the **Generate** button:

This generates the report shown in the following screenshot. It has the list of test cases added under the selected test cycle. In our case, we have the `TESTP-T2` test case, which has been executed a total four times as a part of test cycle `TESTP-C1`. The **Status** column indicates its status during each execution, and there are other columns that give other details:

Test execution results (list)

Key	Name	Status	Actual End Date	Estimated	Actual	Assigned to	Executed by	Environment	Test Cycle	Issues	T
TESTP-E11	TESTP-T2 (1.0) - TM_Education Loan Login Test	PASS	20/Jan/19 8:30 Pm	00:00	00:00	Atar.Afsana@Consulseer.In	Atar.Afsana@Consulseer.In		TESTP-C1		👤
TESTP-E10	TESTP-T2 (1.0) - TM_Education Loan Login Test	BLOCKED	20/Jan/19 8:30 Pm	00:00	00:00	Atar.Afsana@Consulseer.In	Atar.Afsana@Consulseer.In		TESTP-C1		👤
TESTP-E9	TESTP-T2 (1.0) - TM_Education Loan Login Test	FAIL	20/Jan/19 8:29 Pm	00:00	00:00	Atar.Afsana@Consulseer.In	Atar.Afsana@Consulseer.In		TESTP-C1		👤
TESTP-E1	TESTP-T2 (1.0) - TM_Education Loan Login Test	FAIL	20/Jan/19 8:28 Pm	00:00	00:00	Atar.Afsana@Consulseer.In	Atar.Afsana@Consulseer.In		TESTP-C1	TESTP-1	👤

Requirement-based reports

Requirement-based reports help us to understand the current execution status for the selected requirement. In the case of projects where there are multiple requirements, these reports are helpful as they group the test cases based on the requirement tickets in Jira. Let's create one using Jira plugins.

synapseRT

synapseRT has an option to generate requirement-based reports and track the progress of the current execution based on requirements:

1. In order to create a requirement-based report in synapseRT, navigate to the **SynapseRT Reports** tab and select the **Requirement Based Reports** option. This lets you customize the report based on requirements. As shown in the following screenshot, enter all the required details along with the **Test Plan**, and it will generate the report to which the selected requirement ticket has been linked:

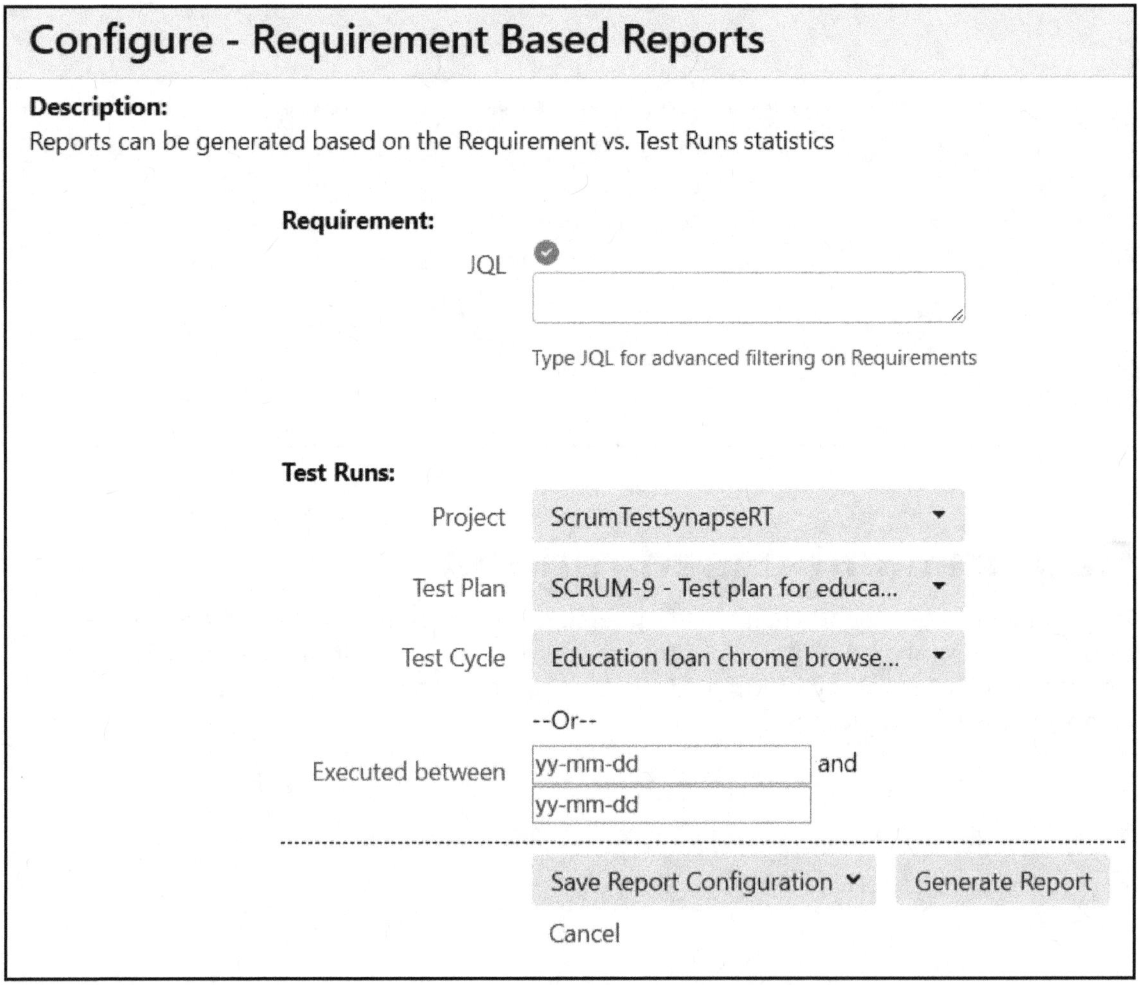

Configure - Requirement Based Reports

Description:
Reports can be generated based on the Requirement vs. Test Runs statistics

Requirement:

JQL ✅

Type JQL for advanced filtering on Requirements

Test Runs:

Project	ScrumTestSynapseRT ▼
Test Plan	SCRUM-9 - Test plan for educa... ▼
Test Cycle	Education loan chrome browse... ▼

--Or--

Executed between | yy-mm-dd | and
| yy-mm-dd |

Save Report Configuration ▼   Generate Report

Cancel

---

2. It generates the report shown in the following screenshot. The graph shows the status of the execution for the selected requirement ticket. It also has the **Summary Report** and **Detailed Report** sections. The **Summary Report** section shows the details such as **Project** name, its **Requirements**, and linked **Test Cases** with their current execution statuses:

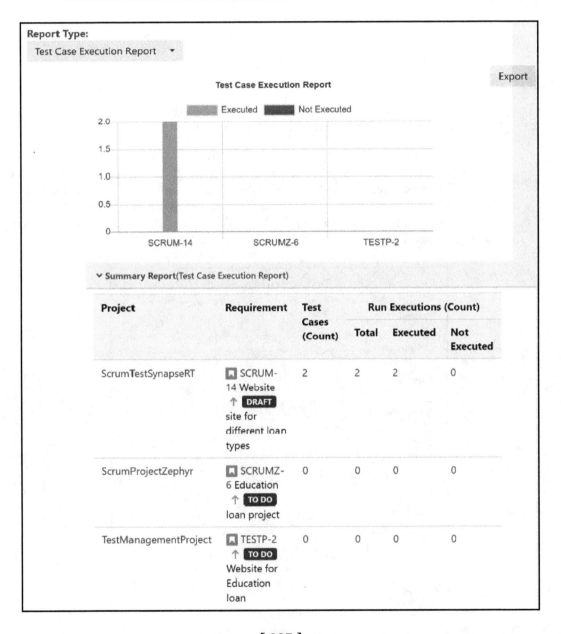

Report Type:

Test Case Execution Report ▾

Export

Test Case Execution Report

◻ Executed   ◼ Not Executed

❮ **Summary Report(Test Case Execution Report)**

Project	Requirement	Test Cases (Count)	Run Executions (Count)		
			Total	Executed	Not Executed
ScrumTestSynapseRT	🔲 SCRUM-14 Website ↑ DRAFT site for different loan types	2	2	2	0
ScrumProjectZephyr	🔲 SCRUMZ-6 Education ↑ TO DO loan project	0	0	0	0
TestManagementProject	🔲 TESTP-2 ↑ TO DO Website for Education loan	0	0	0	0

The **Detailed Report** section shows details about the selected requirement and its linked **Test Cases**, **Test Cycle**, and **Result** of the execution.

Zephyr

Zephyr doesn't have a feature to generate requirement-based reports.

Test Management

The Test Management tool uses the test execution results by coverage report, which indicates the current status of the test cases based on the linked requirements:

1. In order to create a test execution results by coverage report, navigate to the **Tests | Reports | Test Execution** tab and select the option as **Test execution results by coverage**. This shows the configuration page to customize the report and generate it as needed. As shown in the following screenshot, on the configuration page, enter the required details, such as **Project**, **Folder**, and **Start date** and **End date**, and click on the **Generate** button:

2. This generates the report shown in the following screenshot. The *y* axis shows the list of user stories and the *x* axis shows the number of the test cases grouped by user stories. The following graph indicates that the TESTP-6 user story has a total of eight test cases linked to it, of which two have been blocked, two have failed, and four have passed:

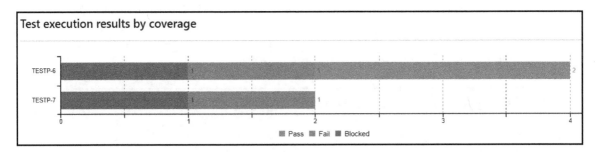

Defect matrix reports

As the name suggests, defect matrix reports can be used to find out the current status of the defects linked to the test cases. Hence, it helps to know the progress of the current test cycle and test plan for the selected project. There are various options for customizing and generating such reports based on the defect's current status, assignee, priority, components, and so on. Let's try to generate a defect matrix report using Jira plugins.

synapseRT

synapseRT has an option to create a defect matrix report and verify the status of the current cycle or test plan execution in terms of the defects reported by the team:

1. In order to generate a defect matrix report in synapseRT, navigate to the **SynapseRT Reports** tab and select the **Defect Matrix Report** option. This shows the option to configure the report. We can also select the way we want to view the report by selecting *x* axis and *y* axis values. After entering all the required details, click on the **Generate Report** button:

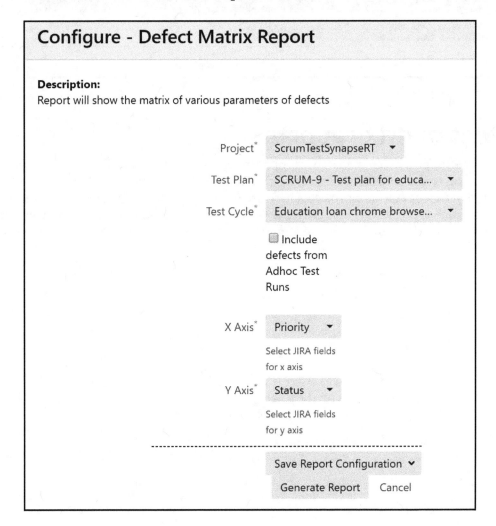

2. The following report is generated, which indicates the defect status in graphical format. As shown in the following screenshot, the selected test cycle has a total of three defects, of which two are of **Medium** priority and one is of **High** priority. It also provides details of the defects, such as its defect number in the **Defect** column and **Resolution**:

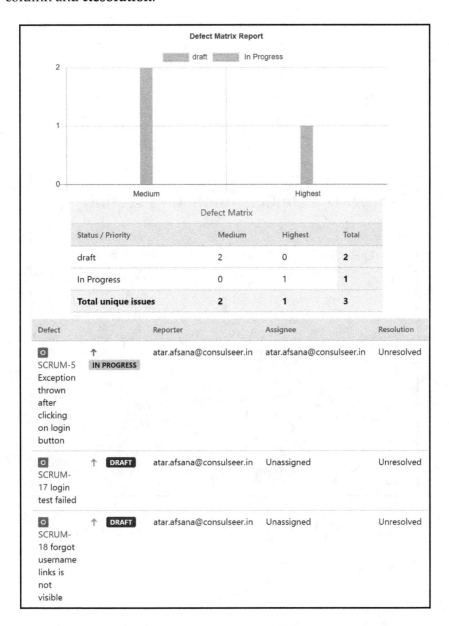

Zephyr

Zephyr doesn't have a feature to generate defect matrix reports. However, it helps us to identify defects that are highly impacting the test execution phase:

1. In order to generate this report, navigate to the **Reports** tab and select the option of **Top Defects Impacting Testing** from the **Other** reports section.

2. To customize the report, enter the required details, enter the number of defects that you want to view, and the status of the defect. Now, as shown in the following screenshot, the number of defects selected is **10** and the status is **draft**. Click on **Next** to generate the report:

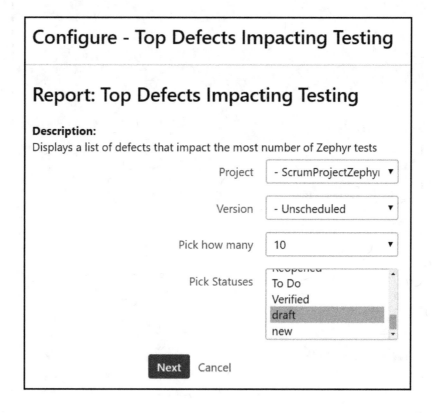

3. The following report gets generated. It lists the **Defect ID**, its **Summary**, **Status**, and **Tests Affected** (the number of test cases affected by each defect). In this case, the project has a total of three defects, of which SCRUMZ-16 is impacting two test cases:

Top Defects Impacting Testing			⚙ Configure
Top Defects Report for ScrumProjectZephyr			
Top 10 Defects			
Defect ID	**Summary**	**Status**	**Tests Affected**
SCRUMZ-12	defect 1	draft	1
SCRUMZ-14	defect 3	draft	1
SCRUMZ-16	defect 5	draft	2

Test Management

Test Management has a Test Execution (Issues) report, which lists all the issues reported during the selected cycle, test plan, version, iteration, or even folder. This report can be generated from the **Reports** tab:

1. In order to create the Test Execution (Issues) report, navigate to the **Tests | Reports | Test Execution** tab. Test Management has added additional reports; however, we can still use the legacy report option to generate the report.
2. Select the **Switch to legacy reports** option to use the legacy report format.
3. Once you switch the view, navigate to the **Test Execution** tab and select the **Test Execution (Issues)** option. As shown in the following screenshot, doing this shows the report configuration page. Enter the required details. Select the test cycle, enter start and end dates, and click on the **Generate** button:

The following report gets generated, which shows the total defects created with their **Priority**, **Status**, and so on:

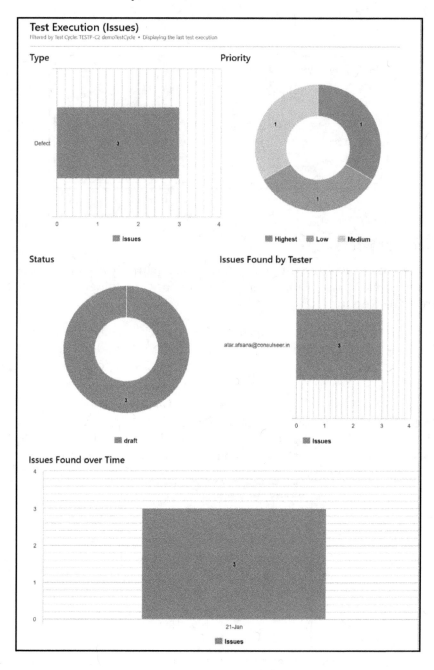

In the **Issues** section, you can also see the defect details, such as the issue ID in the **Key** column and **Summary**:

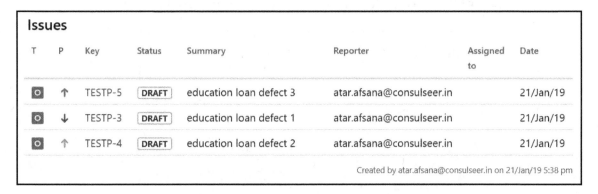

Test suite report

If the test cases are added and executed based on test suites, then it's good to generate test execution reports based on the test suite. This gives details about the current execution status of the test cases, who has executed them, and who the responsible tester is. Let's generate this report using Jira plugins.

synapseRT

synapseRT has an option to generate test suite reports, with the help of which test suite progress can be tracked:

1. In order to generate a test suite report in synapseRT, navigate to the **SynapseRT Reports** tab and select the **Test Suite Report** option. This gives you the options to configure a report based on the **Project**, **Test Suite**, **Test Plan**, **Test Cycle**, and so on.

2. Enter data in all the required fields and click on the **Generate Report** button. As shown in the following screenshot, we have provided details about the **Project**, **Test Suite**, and **Test Plan** in which these test cases have been added:

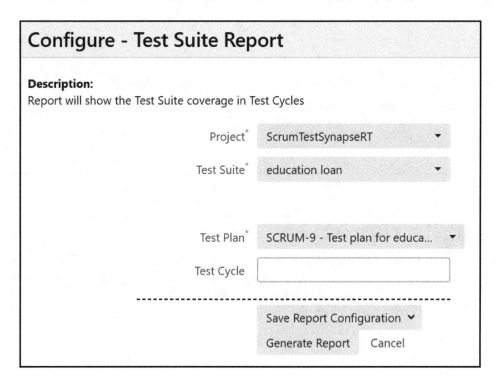

This generates the report shown in the following screenshot. The report has sections such as those to do with test suite coverage and search details. The **Test Suite Coverage** section indicates the total number of test cases and their current status for the selected cycle.

The **Cycle and Run details** indicate the test cycles under which these test cases have been added and their current execution status and other details. This report also lists all the defects linked to these test cases:

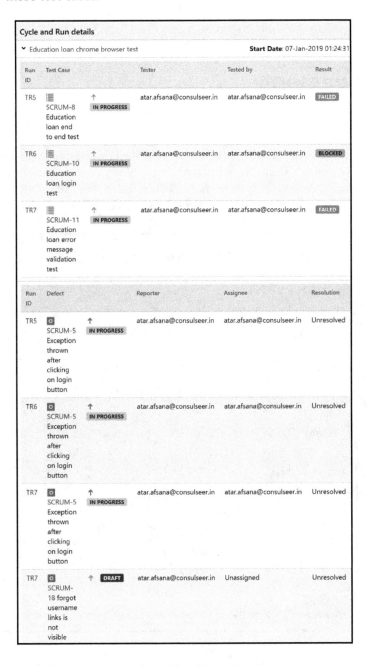

Zephyr

Zephyr doesn't have a feature to generate test suite reports. However, we can still view the status of the executed tests for the selected test cycle, as shown in the preceding Zephyr ad hoc test run report for the ad hoc test cycle.

Test Management

Test Management has a folder structure for organizing test cases, hence when generating a report based on a test suite, we will have to select the option based on the folder:

1. In order to generate the test suite report in Test Management, navigate to the **Tests | Reports | Test Execution** tab and enter the required details. As shown in the following screenshot, enter the project name, the **Folder** (test suite) for which a report needs to be generated, and so on, and click on the **Generate** button:

2. This generates the report shown in the following screenshot. It lists details such as the folder name for which this report has been created, the total number of test cases, and their execution statuses. It also indicates the percentage of the test cases in any given status. In this case, we have **33.33%** of test cases in the **Pass** status. It also shows details regarding how much of the test execution is remaining, has been **Completed**, and so on. The **Issues** section lists defects linked to the test cases, if any:

Folder		Test Execution Results								Effort				Issues		
	Total	Not Executed	In Progress	Pass	Fail	Blocked	Completed	Remaining	Progress	Estimated	Actual	Remaining	Variation	Open	Closed	Total
TestManagementProject/Education Loan	9	0% (0)	0% (0)	33.33% (3)	33.33% (3)	33.33% (3)	9	0	100%	00:00	00:00	00:00	-	0	0	0
Total	9	0% (0)	0% (0)	33.33% (3)	33.33% (3)	33.33% (3)	9	0	100%	00:00	00:00	00:00	-	0	0	0

Burndown chart

A test case burndown chart helps a project team to track the rate of the execution of the test cases for the selected test cycle. It also indicates the number of the test cases that have been executed for the selected date, week, or month, and the remaining test cases. It helps a team to know how much more effort is required to finish the selected test cycle. Let's create this report with the help of Jira plugins.

synapseRT

synapseRT has an option to generate a test case burndown report, which can be used to track the rate of test execution:

1. In order to generate a test case burndown report in the synapseRT tool, navigate to the **SynapseRT Reports** section and select the **Test Case Burndown Report** option. This lets you choose the **Project**, **Test Plan**, and **Test Cycles** for which the report must be generated.
2. As shown in the following screenshot, enter all the required details, then click on the **Generate Report** button:

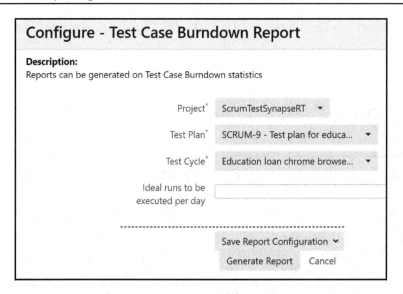

3. This generates the test case burndown report, as shown in the following screenshot. The x axis indicates the number of test cases and the y axis indicates the dates on which these test cases were executed. As shown in the following screenshot, the execution start date is **Jan 7** and last date of the execution is **Jan 22**, as that's the date when this report was generated:

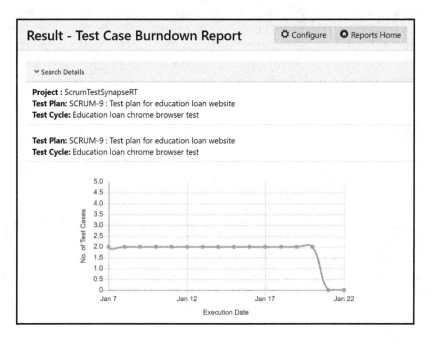

4. If we hover the mouse on a node, it provides further details, such as the date and the remaining number of test cases that need to be executed. As shown in the following screenshot, the selected node has a date of **January 17, 2019**, and there are two test cases that were yet to be executed as of that day:

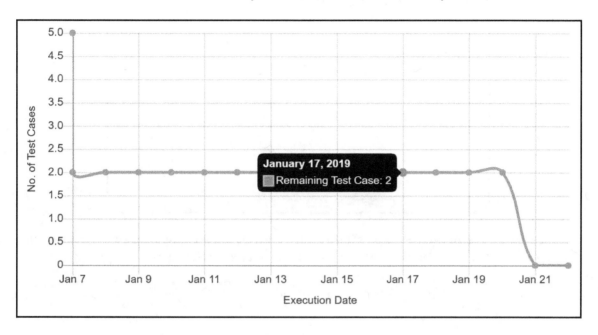

Zephyr

Zephyr has an option to generate a test execution burndown chart, which helps a team to understand the status of the current test execution phase:

1. In order to create this report, navigate to the **Reports** section and select the option as **Test Execution Burndown Chart** from the **Other** section of the reports. Enter the details, as shown in the following screenshot, to generate the test execution burndown chart for all the cycles:

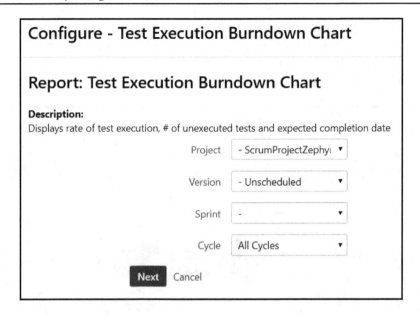

This generates the following graph. The graph indicates the **Average rate of execution**, the **Total unexecuted tests remaining,** and the **Expected completion date**:

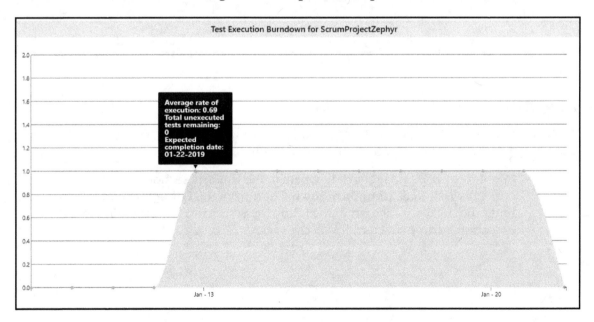

In this case, these values are as follows:

- **Average rate of execution**: 0.69
- **Total unexecuted tests remaining**: 0
- **Expected completion date**: 01-22-2019

Test Management

Test Management has an option to generate a test execution burndown chart, with the help of which the rate of test execution can be tracked:

1. In order to generate a test execution burndown chart in the Test Management tool, navigate to the **Tests | Reports | Test execution** tab, and select the **Test execution burn down** option. This shows the configuration page.
2. Enter the details, select the duration of the report, and click on the **Generate** button:

3. This generates the following report, which indicates the rate of the daily execution of the test cases for the two selected test cycles. The y axis indicates the total number of the test cases and the x axis shows the days on which these test cases were executed:

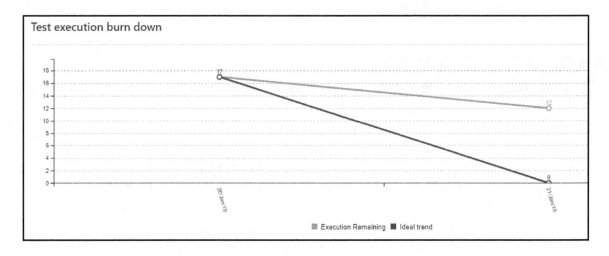

Summary

In this chapter, we learned how to create various reports using Jira plugins, and understood the purpose for each type. We saw how reports help in monitoring and controlling testing activities.

As we know, reporting serves as a great communication tool to provide insights about a project throughout the project development life cycle. Hence, it is essential that the project team and management understand its importance and find ways to utilize essential reports for their projects appropriately.

In the next chapter, we will explore how third-party automated testing tools can be integrated with Jira to manage automated test cases.

6
Section 6: Continuous Integration with Jira and Jenkins

We are going to learn about how Jira can help an SQA team to utilize a DevOps pipeline to automate the execution and management of test cases. We will learn how to configure Jira with Jenkins to execute automated test cases in Selenium.

This section will include the following chapter:

- Chapter 11, *Jira Integration with Automated Testing Tools*

11
Jira Integration with Automated Testing Tools

In the previous chapters, we have learned what test management is and how Jira helps SQA teams manage the testing process effectively. Now, let's see how Jira and the DevOps pipeline can be leveraged to automate and manage test execution to improve agility in the development life cycle.

In this chapter, we will cover the following topics:

- Understanding the DevOps pipeline
- Configuring Jira plugins to connect to Jenkins
- Understanding an example workflow to integrate and execute automated scripts

We will also learn how Jira helps with **continuous integration** (**CI**) and **continuous delivery** (**CD**) in a software project.

Understanding the DevOps pipeline

DevOps is a software development paradigm that involves a cycle of continuous development, testing, integration, deployment, and monitoring. This model is the result of maturing software development practices, especially with the advent of the Agile methodologies, which require faster product and service releases while ensuring adequate quality measures. The following diagram shows the stages in the DevOps cycle:

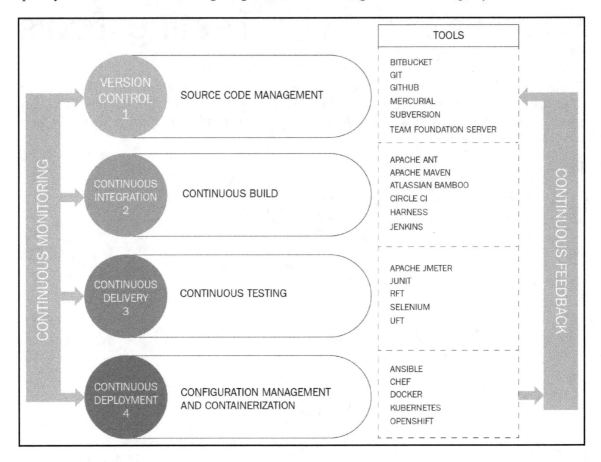

As you can see in the preceding diagram, DevOps requires development, testing, and operations' functions to act in tandem. DevOps phases are basically an automated and streamlined implementation of the development phase in the Agile SDLC.

In the development phase, developers start writing code based on the requirements for the product. Also, testers start writing test cases or scripts for automated testing. This requires developers and testers to make several commits of their artifacts while maintaining several versions of their code and scripts before a final working build can be achieved. Hence, source code management is essential for effective and productive development. This can be problematic in a team environment without a version control tool. Hence, DevOps employs several version controlling tools, such as GitHub, Bitbucket, and Team Foundation.

Once the developer commits the code, the DevOps processes get triggered, which automatically compiles and builds the code along with the other set of code commits from the rest of the team. If proper unit tests have been written, DevOps processes and then executes them to assert whether the results match expectations. Any defects or issues found at this stage are communicated through emails and tickets to the development team. There are several tools on the market for CI, such as Jenkins and Circle CI. We will be looking at utilizing Jenkins with Jira in this chapter. Jenkins is an open source tool for CI. It can be integrated with several software development tools to automate the process of CI/CD.

Once the build passes the unit tests and integration tests at the development level, the release build is deployed to appropriate testing servers for the testing team to initiate their tests. At this point, automation test scripts (if available) are triggered to test the build. Automation ensures that the DevOps phases are continuous; otherwise, it leads to bottlenecks in the agility of the development process. There are several test automation frameworks and tools available, such as Selenium, TestComplete, and Eggplant, which can help to automate the testing process.

The build, once it is tested and fixed for all defects, is then ready to be deployed. After appropriate approvals from the product team and stakeholders, it is then deployed to the production server. Containerization of deployed builds helps facilitate resilient servers, as well as effective load balancing and configuration management. Numerous containerization tools are available on the market, including Docker, Ansible, and Kubernetes.

All phases of the DevOps process require continuous monitoring, using tools such as Prometheus, Splunk, and Ganglia, to alert the development teams to issues that need to be resolved efficiently. Continuous monitoring is necessary for addressing bottlenecks and improving processes for a faster delivery mechanism. Continuous feedback is another mechanism that improves the product by helping the team plan for the next deployment.

Now that we understand the basics of the DevOps process, let's see how we can configure Jenkins to integrate it with Jira and test automation tools.

Configuring Jira plugins to connect to Jenkins

Each of the synapseRT, Zephyr, and Test Management tools for Jira plugins have their own way of connecting with CI/CD tools, such as Jenkins. We will be looking at how to install and configure each of these Jira plugins for Jenkins.

synapseRT

synapseRT comes pre-installed with integration with CI/CD tools. Let's configure the plugin to connect to our Jenkins installation:

1. Go to **Administration** | **Add-ons** | **synapseRT** | **Integration** and click on the **Add** button.
2. Set **Jenkins** as the **Type** of application and provide the Jenkins URL. In our case, we have hosted Jira on a Docker instance, while Jenkins is hosted on the localhost at port `8081`. Hence, we provide `http://host.docker.internal:8081` as the URL instead of `http://localhost:8081`, along with the **User** and **Password** for the Jenkins instance:

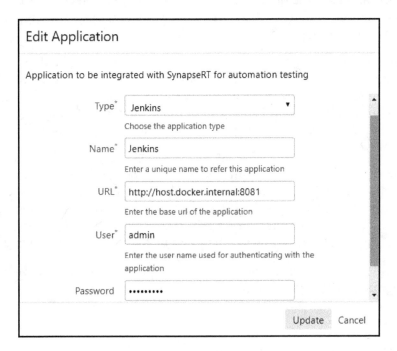

For more information or clarification on issues regarding configuring and setting up synapseRT for Jenkins, visit `https://bit.ly/2RBEAfA`.

Zephyr

Zephyr provides plugins for integrating with Jenkins:

1. To install the plugin, click on **Manage Jenkins** | **Manage Plugins**:

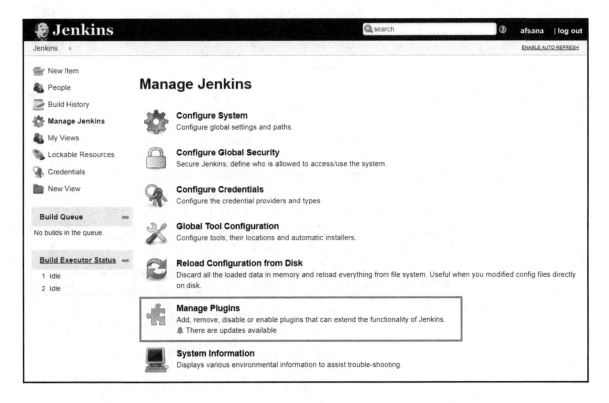

2. Click on the **Available** tab, search for `Zephyr for Jira`, and click on either the **Install without restart** or the **Download now and install after restart** button. Once installed successfully, the plugin will be visible on the **Installed** tab:

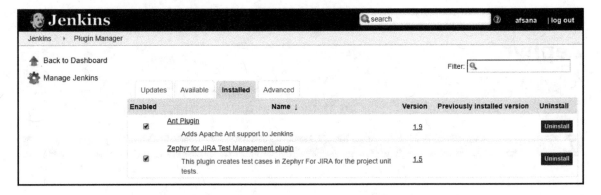

Once it's installed, we can configure the plugin to connect it with Zephyr for Jira in our instance of Jira.

3. Now, click on **Manage Jenkins** and click on **Configure System**. If the plugin was installed correctly, the **Configure System** will have a section, **Zephyr For JIRA - Test Management Configuration**. Select the type of Jira instance in your organization. In our case, we select the **JIRA Server/Data Center**.

4. Provide the **JIRA Server** URL and the credentials that are connected to the projects in Jira. Click on the **Test Configuration** button to validate the settings. If everything is validated, it will look like this:

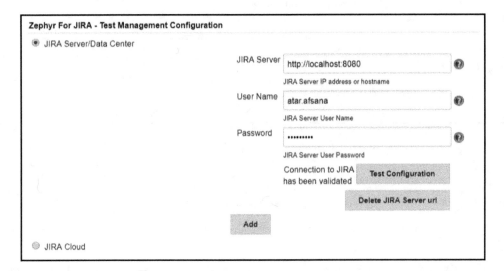

For more information or clarification on issues regarding configuring and setting up Zephyr for Jira for Jenkins, visit the following link: `https://wiki.jenkins.io/display/JENKINS/Zephyr+For+Jira+Test+Management+Plugin`.

Test Management

Test Management for Jira provides plugins for integrating with Jenkins.

1. To install the plugin, click on **Manage Jenkins** | **Manage Plugins**, just as you did for Zephyr.
2. Then, click on the **Available** tab, search for `Test Management for Jira`, and click on either the **Install without restart** or the **Download now and install after restart** button. Once installed successfully, the plugin will be visible on the **Installed** tab:

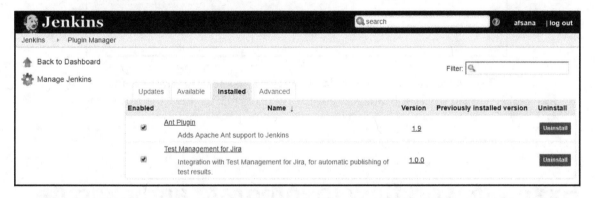

3. Once it's installed, we can configure the plugin to connect it with Test Management for Jira in our instance of Jira. Click on **Manage Jenkins** and click on **Configure System**. If the plugin was installed correctly, the configure system will have a section as **Test Management for Jira**. Select the type of Jira instance in your organization. In our case, we select the **Jira Server(s)**.

4. Provide the **Jira URL** and the credentials that are connected to the projects in Jira. Click on the **Test Configuration** button to validate the settings. If everything is validated, it will look like this:

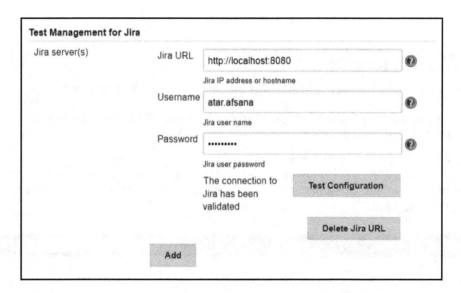

 For more information or clarification on issues regarding configuring and setting up Test Management for Jira for Jenkins, visit the following link: https://www.adaptavist.com/doco/display/KT/Jenkins.

Example workflow to integrate and execute automated scripts

Now that we have configured our plugins to integrate with Jenkins, we now see an example of how the DevOps pipeline functions with each plugin. For this workflow, we use the following automated test script:

1. Create a test automation code in Eclipse with a TestNG build script in XML. For this purpose, we have created the code in Java using Eclipse. We have created a new Java project in a new package named JenkinsDemoPkg with a class named demoJenkins. We also use JenkinsDemoPkg.demoJenkins: testJenkins to get the complete name of the class and method, which will be used for tracking in plugins:

```
package JenkinsDemoPkg;
import org.testng.annotations.Test;
public class demoJenkins {
        @Test
        public void testJenkins(){
                System.out.println("Hello World");
        }
}
```

Now, right-click on the Java class file and select **Convert to TestNG** from the
TestNG context menu. The TestNG plugin needs to be installed on Eclipse
via **Help | Install New Software...** to get the TestNG context menu:

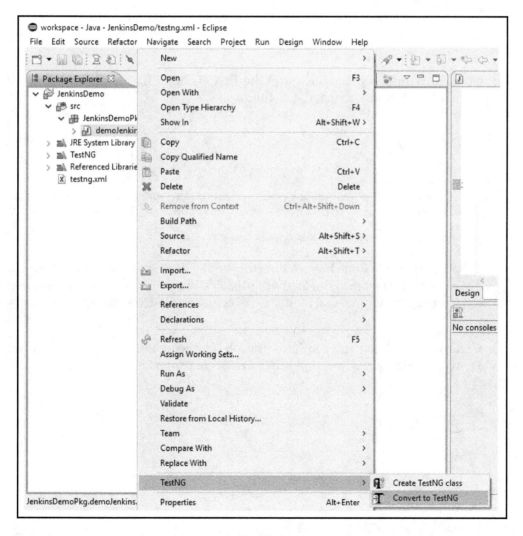

This creates an XML file as follows:

```
<?xml version="1.0" encoding="UTF-8"?>
<!DOCTYPE suite SYSTEM "http://testng.org/testng-1.0.dtd">
<suite name="Suite">
  <test thread-count="5" name="Test">
    <classes>
      <class name="JenkinsDemoPkg.demoJenkins"/>
    </classes>
  </test> <!-- Test -->
</suite> <!-- Suite -->
```

 The project has been placed in the
`C:\Users\Owner\workspace\JenkinsDemo` directory.

2. Create a Windows batch file to run the TestNG build file. To execute this build, we use the Windows batch file as follows:

```
@echo off
rem run.bat
c:
cd C:\Users\Owner\workspace\JenkinsDemo
set
classpath=C:\Users\Owner\workspace\JenkinsDemo\bin;C:\Users\Owner\.
p2\pool\plugins\*;C:\Users\Owner\Desktop\Projects\seleniumtest\lib\
*;
java org.testng.TestNG testng.xml
```

The batch file first changes directory to the location of the project and then sets the classpath. The classpath is basically the path where your libraries are stored for the project. Finally, we execute the TestNG project using the XML file.

3. Create a Jenkins job and configure the job to execute the code. Click on **New Item**, provide a job name, and select **Freestyle project**:

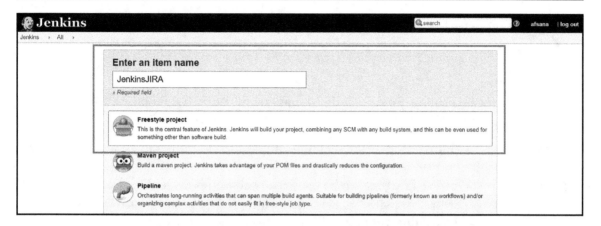

Let's configure the job by clicking on **Configure**. Now provide the project directory as a custom workspace:

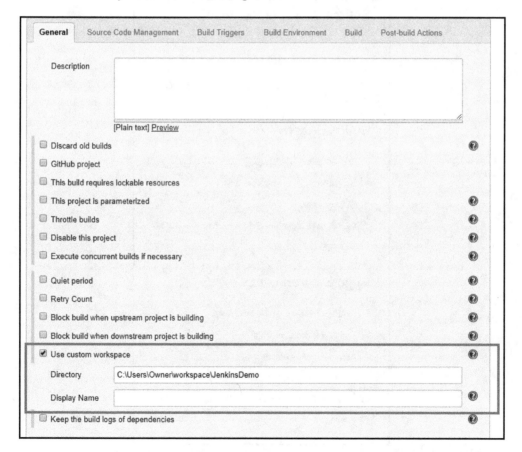

Steps 1 to 3 will remain the same for all plugins.

4. The next sections (**Source Code Management**, **Build Triggers**, and **Build Environment**) can be used as required in your project:

   • **Source Code Management** can be used to pull your code from version control tools such as Git and GitHub.
   • **Build Triggers** can be used to specify how the Jenkins job will be triggered. Jenkins jobs can be triggered in a variety of ways.
   • **Build Environment** allows us to configure the environment to execute the job:

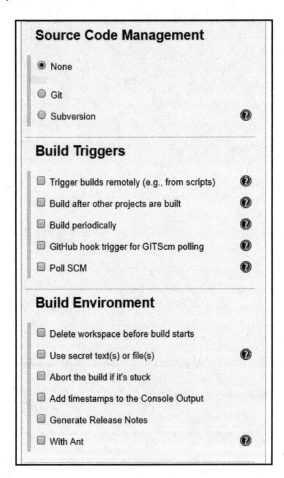

5. Now, provide the name of the Windows batch file we created in the build section and click **OK**:

synapseRT

Let's see the steps to integrate Jenkins with synapseRT.

1. Capture the results of the build action as a post-build activity. To capture the results of the build in Jenkins so that synapseRT can pull them, the **Post-build Actions** need to be configured for the Jenkins job as follows:

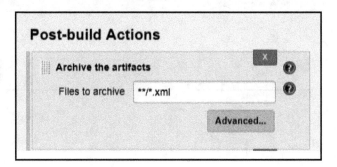

2. synapseRT allows us to trigger the Jenkins job from within the test cycle. For synapseRT to be able to track the execution results, it needs the **Test Reference** to be added to the test case in the **Automation** section:

3. The **Automation | Test Reference** is the complete name of the module we captured in step 1. Then, add the test case to a test cycle and click on the **Run** button to trigger the Jenkins job:

When you click the **Run** button, the Jenkins job starts running:

4. Capture the result of the build in the Jira plugin. After around 60 seconds, the results of the job will be captured in Jira:

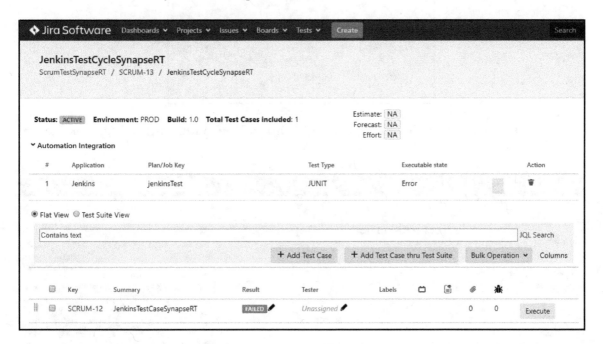

Zephyr

Let's see the steps to integrate Jenkins with Zephyr.

1. Capture the results of the build action as a post-build activity. To capture the results of the build in Jenkins so that Zephyr can pull it, the **Post-build Actions** need to be configured for the Jenkins job. Provide the **Project Name** for the Zephyr project and select the appropriate **Cycle** and **Version**:

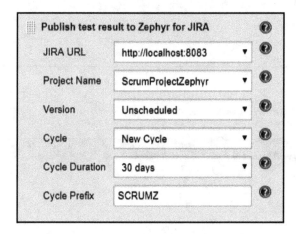

2. To trigger the Jenkins job, click on the **Build Now** button after clicking on the job name:

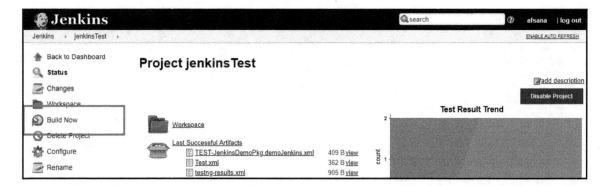

3. Capture the result of the build in the Jira plugin. After the Jenkins job completes, the result will be captured in the post-build activity and sent to Zephyr in Jira. The result of the build is captured in Zephyr:

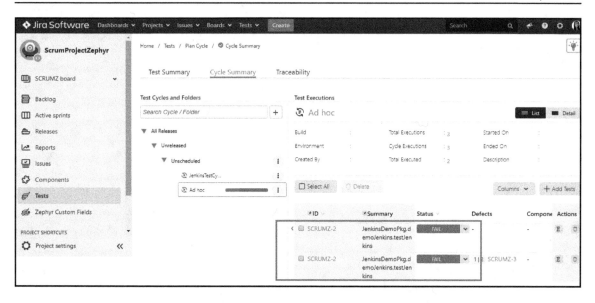

Test Management

Integrating Test Management for Jira with Jenkins and other CI/CD tools is like the setup we performed for Zephyr. This has been covered in detail in the help section at the following link: `https://www.adaptavist.com/doco/display/KT/Integrations`.

Summary

In this chapter, we learned about the DevOps pipeline and execution using Jira plugins. We learned how the DevOps pipeline can be leveraged in a software development project to become truly agile and deliver continuously, while improving in making deliveries. We configured our Test Management plugins for Jira to integrate with Jenkins as our CI/CD tool. We saw a simple hands-on example of working in the DevOps pipeline for automating test case management.

Here comes the end of our long journey. I hope you enjoyed reading this book!

Other Books You May Enjoy

If you enjoyed this book, you may be interested in these other books by Packt:

Hands-On Agile Software Development with JIRA
David Harned

ISBN: 978-1-78953-213-5

- Create your first project (and manage existing projects) in JIRA
- Manage your board view and backlogs in JIRA
- Run a Scrum Sprint project in JIRA
- Create reports (including topic-based reports)
- Forecast using versions
- Search for issues with JIRA Query Language (JQL)
- Execute bulk changes to issues
- Create custom filters, dashboards, and widgets
- Create epics, stories, bugs, and tasks

Jira Software Essentials - Second Edition
Patrick Li

ISBN: 978-1-78883-351-6

- Understand the basics and agile methodologies of Jira software
- Use Jira Software in a Scrum environment
- Manage and run Jira Software projects beyond the out of box Scrum and Kanban way
- Combine Scrum and Kanban and use other project management options beyond just agile
- Customize Jira Software's various features and options as per your requirements
- Work with Jira Agile offline, and plan and forecast projects with agile portfolio
- Integrate Jira Agile with Confluence and Bitbucket

Leave a review - let other readers know what you think

Please share your thoughts on this book with others by leaving a review on the site that you bought it from. If you purchased the book from Amazon, please leave us an honest review on this book's Amazon page. This is vital so that other potential readers can see and use your unbiased opinion to make purchasing decisions, we can understand what our customers think about our products, and our authors can see your feedback on the title that they have worked with Packt to create. It will only take a few minutes of your time, but is valuable to other potential customers, our authors, and Packt. Thank you!

Index

I

Improving Performance (IMP) 27
integration testing 38
International Organization for Standardization
    (ISO) 10
ISO 9000 series 20, 21, 24

J

Jenkins
  integrating, with synapseRT 237, 239
  integrating, with Zephyr 240
Jira issue type
  creating, as requirement 179
Jira plugins
  configuring, for connecting to Jenkins 228
  used, for creating defects 164
  used, for creating test plan 109, 110, 111
  used, for establishing relations between
    requirements and test cases 185
  used, for establishing relations between
    requirements and test plan 119
  used, for organizing test plan 109, 110, 111
Jira
  about 45, 55
  Agile project management 46
  defect workflows, creating 166, 167, 168
  functionalities 46
  Kanban project, creating 55
  project, managing 50
  projects, initiating 50, 51
  projects, organizing 46
  role-based permissions 52
  Scrum project, creating 53, 54

K

Kanban project
  about 50
  creating, in Jira 55

L

load testing 39
logging defects
  cons 162
  pros 162

M

Managing Business Resilience (MBR) 26
Managing the Workforce (MWF) 27
maturity levels 28, 29
meetings, Scrum
  backlog refinement meeting 49
  daily scrum 50
  sprint planning 49
  sprint retrospective 49
  sprint review 49

P

performance testing 38
permissions, Jira
  global permission 52
  issue security permission 52
  project permission 52
Plan-Do-Check-Act (PDCA) 23
Planning and Managing Work (PMW) 26
Product Backlog Item (PBI) 49
Product Risk Analysis (PRA) 110
project administrator 52
project requisites organization, Scrum
  Product Backlog 48
  Sprint Backlog 49
projects
  initiating, in Jira 51
  organizing, with Jira 46

Q

Quality Assurance (QA) 15
Quality Management System (QMS)
  about 19
  CMMI 25, 27
  ISO 9000 series 20, 21, 24
  maturity levels 28, 29
quality
  about 10, 12, 15
  ensuring 16, 17
  significance 15, 16

R

regression testing 39
reports

www.ingramcontent.com/pod-product-compliance
Lightning Source LLC
LaVergne TN
LVHW081520050326
832903LV00025B/1564